Daniel Cooledge Fletcher

**Reminiscences of California and the Civil War**

Daniel Cooledge Fletcher

**Reminiscences of California and the Civil War**

ISBN/EAN: 9783337219734

Printed in Europe, USA, Canada, Australia, Japan

Cover: Foto ©ninafisch / pixelio.de

More available books at **www.hansebooks.com**

# REMINISCENCES

—OF—

# CALIFORNIA

—AND THE—

# CIVIL WAR

—BY—

## DANIEL COOLEDGE FLETCHER.

SERGT. CO. H, 40TH REGT., N. Y. V.

---

AYER, MASS.:
PRESS OF HUNTLEY S. TURNER.
1894.

# PREFACE.

For quite a number of years I have been requested by my friends, especially by my niece, to write an account of my experiences in California and the War. I have not done so until quite lately, however, since I have not been accustomed to writing.

Most of the following pages have been written during the last few winters, when I have been compelled by the severity of the weather to remain in the house. The more I have written, the more I have become interested in the subject, and I have found the work a great deal of company, especially during the cold winter season, when I have had much leisure.

My sufferings and sacrifices for my country must be my apology for intruding upon the kindness of my friends. Then, too, I have hoped that my travels and adventures, which are perhaps out of the ordinary run, might prove of interest to many.

The idea of writing a book was partly suggested by a pamphlet I saw a few years ago, written in memory of a friend of mine, who lost an arm at Gettysburg, and died shortly after the War from the effects of the wound. At first my purpose was simply to commit to writing a few facts of my life, somewhat after the manner of this pamphlet; but one thought suggested another, until finally the following pages were written.

DANIEL C. FLETCHER.

# CONTENTS.

## CHAPTER I.
### JOURNEY TO CALIFORNIA.

Description of different routes to California. Start for California. First night on board ship. On the wide ocean. Sea sickness. Near the Bahama Banks. First stopping place, Kingston, Jamaica. Description of Jamaica. Arrival at Chagres. Journey up the Chagres River. Arrival at Gargano. From Gargano to Panama. Description of Panama. On the Pacific Ocean. Ocean very calm. Whale ship spoken. Steamer stopped for what was supposed to be a wreck. Arrival at Acapulco. On shore for dinner. A person found destitute and provided for. Leave Acapulco. Arrival at San Francisco. Take a steamer for Sacramento. Take another for Marysville. Letter sent home. Start for Nevada City. Arrival at Grass Valley.

## CHAPTER II.
### FIRST EXPERIENCES IN MINING.

Description of Grass Valley. First work done in California. Trees blown down in Grass Valley. Stop mining and go to work by the month, at one hundred dollars and board. Wages reduced. At work for eighty dollars. Mining very uncertain business. At work for the Day Company. At work splitting shingles. At work sinking shafts by the foot. Famine in Grass Valley. Men arrive in Grass Valley destitute. Grizzly bear killed between Grass Valley and Rough and Ready. Provisions arrive. End of the famine. Mills at work. Business good again. Indians of Grass Valley. Indian fandango.

## CHAPTER III.

### DESCRIPTION OF THE MINES.

Grass Valley slide. Eureka slide. Grass Valley ravine. Boston ravine. Woodpecker ravine. Surface and deep mines. Pike Flat. Description of a sluice box. Panning out. Cleaning up the gold. Day Mining Company. Gold specimen found by the Day Company worth five hundred dollars  Situation of the quartz mines. Grass Valley the richest quartz mining place in the country. The Allison ledge the richest ledge that was ever discovered. Lafayette ledge. Gold hill. Massachusetts hill. Ophir hill. Church hill. Osborn hill. Quartz mining uncertain. Lead lost and found in Gold hill richer than ever. Description of an incline shaft. Prospecting a quartz ledge. Ledge run out. Union hill quartz ledge a failure.

## CHAPTER IV.

### MINING IN GRASS VALLEY.

Bought into the Point Mining Company. Description of the Point Mining Company. Miners' life. Discouraged miners at work for the company. Second year in California. Living in a cabin twelve feet square. Have letters from home once a month. Buy a steamer edition of the Boston Journal. Gold and silver the money of California. The minister gave us a call. Orthodox fair in aid of the church. Episcopal fair. Sudden departure of the minister. Diabolical actions of the Episcopal minister. Receive letter from my brother Sherman at Downieville. Arrival of my brothers Sherman and Edward across the plains. Profits of driving cattle and horses across the plains to California. Sherman meets an old college mate. Sherman goes to Nevada City to study law with William M. Stewart.

## CHAPTER V.

### DEPARTURE FOR HOME.

Fall of 1853. Sold out the Point claims. Bid good bye to our brothers, partners and acquaintances. Departure for home. Arrival in San Francisco. Buy second cabin tickets. Three steamers start from San Francisco, all in opposition. On the Pacific Ocean. Steamer had a hot box. Arrival at Nicaragua. Across the country to Greytown. Departure for home. Betting on the steamer as to which would arrive in New York first. Steamship race. Arrival in New York first. At home in 1854. Tree speculation. Second trip to California. Arrival in Grass Valley. Sherman District Attorney of Nevada County. Shady Creek mines. First picnic in California. Large attendance at picnic.

## CHAPTER VI.

### NEVADA FIRE. EXPERIENCES IN MINING.

Water gives out at Grass Valley. Prospecting on Deer Creek. Nevada fire, July 19, 1856. Death of Sherman in a fire proof building. Description of the building. Funeral of Sherman. Journey to San Francisco to procure a monument for brother's grave. Letter from Senator Stewart. Engaged in putting in a cut at Shady Creek. Blasting accident. Partner badly injured. A year getting well. Shady Creek cut finished. Return to Grass Valley. Sickness. Mr. Tweed invited me to go up to his house. Soon recover under the care of Mrs. Tweed. At work on my claims at Grass Valley. $269 quartz specimen found. Trip to Shady Creek with the big specimen. Upper claims at Grass Valley jumped. Succeed in getting the intruders off the ground. Let the dispute out to three men to settle. Partner not satisfied with the arrangement.

## CHAPTER VII.

### LAST DAYS IN CALIFORNIA.

Trip to Dutch Flat. Object of going to California. Dispose of my mining claims. Prospect a quartz ledge at Omega. Live in a deserted cabin. Run a tunnel into the hill. Dispute about slavery. Rock out of the tunnel destroying a flume below us. Water carried from the head waters of the South Yuba to Nevada and Grass Valley. Grizzly bear caught in a trap. Stop work on the tunnel. Second trip to Dutch Flat to see friends. Start for home. Brother Edward decides to stop longer. Meet an old schoolmate in San Francisco. Bought through ticket by way of Panama. Voyage to Panama. One of the passengers was on the ship Independence when it was burned. Narrow escape from shipwreck. Arrival at Panama. Across the Isthmus. Arrival home. Account of Edward's enlistment. His death.

# PART SECOND.

## THE WAR OF THE REBELLION.

## CHAPTER VIII.

### ENLISTMENT 1861.

Patriotism of the North. The Selectmen urge the young men to enlist. They did their duty. Joined the

11th Massachusetts Regiment at Boston. Leave the 11th Regiment. Join a company in West Cambridge (now Arlington.) The company went to church Sunday in the Unitarian, Orthodox and Baptist churches, on invitation. No vacancy for a company in a Massachusetts regiment. Start to join a regiment in Brooklyn, New York. Brooklyn regiment not ready. Ordered to return to Massachusetts. Start to join a regiment in Yonkers, New York. Join the 40th Regiment, New York, recruiting at Yonkers. In camp for the first time. Sworn into the United States service 27th June, 1861. Appointed corporal June 28, 1861. Visit from Mayor Wood of New York at midnight. The ladies of Yonkers treat the regiment to strawberries and cream. The regiment starts for Washington, July 4, 1861. Arrival at Washington. First battle of Bull Run. The regiment guard the City of Alexandria.

## CHAPTER IX.

### CAMP LIFE AROUND WASHINGTON IN 1861.

In camp Sacket at Alexandria. On picket for the first time. Disloyal persons found. Ignorance of the poor whites. On reserve picket at a large plantation house. Review of the army by the President, General McClellan and others. Pickets doubled. Visit from my brother. Addison Gage called to see the company. Captain Ingalls had a visit from his wife and child. Our regiment went out with a large scouting party. Return at two in the morning. Our colonel put under arrest for disobeying orders. Colonel in command of his regiment again. Captain Ingalls put under arrest for a week. In command of his company again. Hard work for volunteers. Officers and men to obey orders. Scouting cavalry fired on. Winter quarters. Winter house. Soldier found asleep on his post. Punishment death. Sham fight. One man wounded. Target practice.

## CHAPTER X.

### THE PENINSULAR CAMPAIGN.

Ordered to have three days' rations and be ready to march at a moment's notice. On the voyage to Fort Monroe. Arrival at Fort Monroe. See the Monitor for the first time. Description of the Monitor. Land in a rain storm. Wet all night. In camp at Fort Monroe. Advance on Yorktown. Siege of Yorktown. Many narrow escapes from death during the siege. Rebels left the fortifications. Men killed and wounded by rebel torpedoes. In the rebel works. Rebel purse found, containing rebel postage stamps, money, pens, and a lock of hair. Advance from Yorktown. Battle of Williamsburg. Defeat of the rebels. Rain storm. Spent the night standing up behind a tree in the storm. Without supper or breakfast. Union troops enter the city. Caring for the wounded at Williamsburg. On the march again. Battle of Fair Oaks. General McClellan arrives. Caring for the wounded. Death of Thompson and Ellis.

## CHAPTER XI.

### THE SEVEN DAYS' FIGHT.

Saw Major Ingalls for the last time. On picket duty all night. No sleep. Private property destroyed by order of the Commanding General. Fight in the woods. Battle of Savage Station. Batteries in retreat. Cavalry ordered to advance. Battle of Charles City Cross Roads. Out of drinking water. Very thirsty. Randolph's Battery lose one gun. Major Ingalls wounded, and taken to Annapolis, Maryland. Fight of Malvern Hill. Supporting Randolph's Battery at Malvern Hill. Before we came to the Hill we marched all night without any water. Three men wounded near me at Malvern Hill. Rebel gun dismounted. Many of our regiment killed and wounded. After the battle. Retreat to Harrison's Landing. No sleep. Rain storm. Scott Hammond gave out. Arrival at Harrison's Landing. On picket.

## CHAPTER XII.

### SECOND BULL RUN AND CHANTILLY.

Ordered to be ready to march at a moment's notice. Departure from Harrison's Landing. Arrival and departure from Yorktown. Arrival at Alexandria in a steamboat. Embark in the cars for Centerville. Go in the cars south from Centerville. With General Pope. Return to Centerville. Cavalry repulsed. Going into the Bull Run fight. Birney's attack. Narrow escape. After the battle. Return to Centerville. Two days at Centerville. Ordered into line for the last time. Rebels between us and Washington. Nice carriage destroyed by the enemy. Battle of Chantilly. Thunder storm. Wounded. Getting to the rear. Saw many wounded. Lieutenant Gould and Orderly Sergeant wounded. All the officers wounded down to the corporals. Taken prisoner. Sanitary Commission found us first. Return to Washington.

## CHAPTER XIII.

### HOSPITAL LIFE.

Arrival in Washington. Ward surgeon said leg would have to be amputated. Head surgeon said he would try to save it. Write to friends at home, asking my brother to come to Washington as soon as possible. Wound does not improve. Many wounded in hospital. Limb amputated. Arrival of my brother. Wound does not heal readily. One soldier dies from eating fruit. Surgeon forbids any more fruit to be brought into the hospital. No appetite. Somewhat better. Sanitary Commission Agents very kind. Sisters of Charity. Moved from Cliffborn·to Lincoln Hospital. Discharged from the army. Departure for home on a bed. Arrival home.

# PART FIRST.

## CALIFORNIA.

### CHAPTER I.

JOURNEY TO CALIFORNIA.

In the early days of the gold discovery in California there were three established routes. One was by way of Cape Horn by sailing vessels, a long and tedious journey, occupying from four to five months and sometimes longer, on account of rough and tempestuous weather. A stop was made at Rio Janeiro in Brazil on the Atlantic coast, and another at Valparaiso in Chili for stores, water, and to leave the mail and passengers.

Another route was by way of the Isthmus of Panama. The steamers usually stopped at Kingston, Jamaica, for coal and to leave the mail and passengers. The landing on the Isthmus was at Chagres, at the mouth of the Chagres River. When the Panama railroad was built, the landing place, or port of entry, was changed to Aspinwall, a town situated a number of miles south of Chagres. This route was considered dangerous on account of the Panama fever and the bad living the steerage passengers were provided with, a large part of the passengers buying steerage tickets. Sometimes steerage passengers bought first cabin tickets after starting on the voyage, as the living was so poor; but I did not. It is my opinion that steerage passengers were purposely given poor fare so that they would buy first cabin tickets, and pay the difference. First cabin tickets cost two and three hundred dollars.

After crossing the Isthmus, the steamer on the other side stopped at Acapulco, in Mexico, and at San Diego in Southern California.

The third route was across the plains, from Missouri to California. This journey took the entire summer. The travellers had to live on bear, buffalo and deer meat, and what provisions they took with them, as there were no towns or stopping places on the route at that time.

In 1853 another route was established, which was called the Nicaragua route. The passengers were landed at Greytown, Nicaragua. They went up the San Juan River to Lake Nicaragua, across the lake in a steamboat, and then travelled about twelve miles to San Juan del Sur on the Pacific. This route was five hundred miles shorter on the Pacific Ocean than the Panama route, and about the same distance on the Atlantic. It took one day longer to cross the Isthmus at Nicaragua than at Panama before the railroad was built, but the travelling was much more pleasant than by either of the other routes.

I came home by way of Nicaragua in 1853, making the journey in twenty-three days and some hours, the shortest trip ever made between New York and San Francisco up to that time. We came home on the steamer Star of the West from Greytown to New York, that same steamer that tried to get provisions to Fort Sumter in 1861.

When gold was discovered in California in 1849, my brother Theodore was very desirous of going. My father objected for several reasons, and especially on account of the dangers of the Panama fever, for he had seen in the papers accounts of many deaths from this disease.

About the first of January, 1852, my brother's business arrangements were such that he bought a ticket for California. Imagine my father's consternation when Theodore came home from Boston with this ticket. The steamer was to start from New York only a few days later. Father asked him if he had bought a ticket for me, also, and receiving an answer in the negative, told him to procure one for me, since he knew I wanted to go. I was not at home at the time. My ticket cost one hundred and eighty dollars, Theodore's one hundred and fifty dollars. As a matter of fact, Theodore had had his ticket in his pocket for a month. Father thought that no one ought to go to California alone, and he was about right. Our tickets were through tickets from New York to San Francisco, by way of the Isthmus of Panama. We had to pay our own way across the Isthmus. We each took a valise of clothing, blankets, and such other things as we thought we should need on the voyage, and started for New York.

Neither of us had had much experience in travelling, and as for me, I had never been out of the state except to New Hampshire to visit my sister. Theodore had been to New York once before.

Arriving in New York we went on board the steamer at once. Every thing looked nice and clean; white sheets were on the beds, and other things to correspond. The government inspectors came on board to see that every thing was all right. But after we got out to sea every thing was changed; the white sheets were removed from the beds, and things did not look as lovely as when we first saw the steamer.

We had to take steerage tickets, as we did not have money enough to buy first cabin tickets, and have something left when we arrived in California. The place where we stopped on board the steamer was composed of bunks, one above another, numbered, so that each passenger knew where he was to sleep. The first night at sea I went below about nine o'clock, and found another man in my berth. I told him he was in my berth, and showed him my number, but could not make him leave. I told some of the crew about it, and they told me to go to the captain, he told me to go to the steward, and the steward told me to wait till morning, as he had gone to bed and could not tend to it. I took my blanket and went on deck, and lay down beside the smokestack, but did not sleep much. Thus passed the first night on board the steamer at sea.

The next morning the steward found me a berth much better than the one I had paid for.

As soon as it was warm enough, about four days after leaving New York, I slept on deck, and most of the steerage passengers did the same, as it was very disagreeable down in the steamer where the steerage passengers slept. Nearly every one was seasick, many not recovering until we reached Jamaica. We performed our ablutions on the guard next to the wheelhouse, on the deck. We were furnished with a bucket and rope to draw the water from the ocean; we were furnished with a basin to wash in. We had to furnish our own towels.

We could tell when we were in the Gulf stream; the water was milk warm. One night while sleeping on deck, I was looking up in the sky, and told my brother the ship was going round and round in a circle and not ahead. I found this out by looking at the stars. We were near the Bahama Banks, and the captain did not think it safe to go ahead until daylight.

The steerage passengers were allowed to go on deck and walk about forward of the wheelhouse. The first cabin passengers were allowed to walk the whole length of the steamer, but on account of the large number of steerage passengers, who were in the way, they seldom found it pleasant to go beyond the wheelhouse. The vessel was crowded with passengers.

Our first stopping place was at Kingston, on the Island of Jamaica, where we stopped for coal, supplies, and to leave the mails. When we first came in sight of the Island, it looked like dark clouds close down to the horizon. Before we came into the harbor of Kingston, a negro pilot came on board to take the steamer up to the wharf.

Many of the passengers went on shore and ate the delicious fruits, such as oranges, pineapples, cocoanuts, bananas, limes, lemons and other fruit, in which the Island abounded. And what oranges! I ate ten before I could stop. They were much better than any I had ever seen in Massachusetts, because they were taken fresh from the trees, I suppose. The fruit was peddled about the streets by boys, girls and old women, who lived on the Island.

The coal was put on board the steamer by negro men and women, in baskets holding about a bushel, which they carried on their heads. I should think there were forty or fifty in all. They were in charge of an overseer, who kept them busy night and day until the steamer was loaded.

We did not go far into the country, as we did not know when the steamer would leave. We saw orange, cocoanut and other trees, which bore the nice fruit, and also some cactus, fifteen or twenty feet in height. I thought the ladies at home would like some to put in their gardens.

Most of the inhabitants of the island of Jamaica were Englishmen and negroes. The negroes did not appear very prosperous, and from what I saw of them I should say they had not improved much since they were liberated from slavery.

The steamer having been supplied with coal, we were ready to go, but the wind blew the steamer back upon the wharf, and the sailors were unable to get the head around, so as to allow the wheels to work. A rope was fastened to a buoy some distance from the ship. A large number of passengers took hold of the rope and pulled her around clear of the wharf. As we were sailing out of the harbor, the steamer struck a schooner, which was anchored near the channel. The shock was great, and many of the passengers, being badly shaken up, were much frightened, thinking the ship was going to sink. No great damage was done, as only the schooner's bowsprit was broken. The steamer got out to sea before dark without any other mishap. Most of the passengers put in a supply of fruit to eat on the voyage. Many were seasick again. We passed our time in playing cards, checkers, and in reading books, most of which had been procured previously in New York. Seasickness is so disagreeable that one does not feel much like doing anything. Nothing worthy of note occurred during the rest of the voyage. The sea was very rough most of the way, making travelling very unpleasant.

In due time our steamer cast anchor about two miles from land, off the town of Chagres. We were landed in row boats by the natives, who came from the town to the ship for us. We paid them a dollar each. The sea was rough, and we found it difficult to get into the boats. Sometimes the boat was ten feet below us; then a big wave would float it up to where we were, and in we jumped. Thinking it very dangerous, I hesitated to go at first, but there was no other way to land. Finally when a big wave brought up the boat, I jumped in, and landed all right, but I was wet through before we reached the shore. We expected the boat would be overturned, so rough was the sea. In the scramble I was separated from my brother. When I arrived near the wharf I was greeted with such cries as, "Where have you been?" "What have you been doing?" etc., from Theodore.

We found there were two ways of crossing the Isthmus. One was to sail up the Chagres River on a small steamer to Gargano, and walk or ride on a mule the rest of the way. The other way was to walk or ride all the way. To Gargano was more than half way. We concluded to take the boat. The boat was crowded. It was about fifty miles across the Isthmus. On our left, as we entered Chagres, there was a big bluff between the town and the ocean, on which was situated a fort, which defended the town. Chagres had a population of about three thousand. It was situated close to the ocean, the wharf being on the right. The inhabitants were mostly Spaniards, or descendants of Spaniards, Indians and negroes. Fruits were peddled about the streets. There were several large stores in the place, kept mostly by Spaniards. Trained parrots and monkeys were plenty outside the buildings and on the piazzas of the hotels. Fruit trees were growing around and in front of the town.

After stopping a few hours in Chagres, we proceded up the river to Gargano. Most of the distance along the river the forest trees grew close to the water, and we could see paths in the openings where the wild beasts came down to drink. At night the steamer was run up to the bank and made fast to a tree. In the night we heard all sorts of noises, different from anything we had ever heard before, made by wild beasts and reptiles. We were about half way to Gargano, when the steamer was disabled. Word was sent to the town, and new boats were procured. While waiting for the boats, we amused ourselves by shooting at the doctor's hat with our pistols; by the way, nearly everybody carried a pistol. The doctor was a dentist, bound for Chili, and accompanied by his wife. His hat was pretty well riddled with pistol balls. He extracted a tooth for my brother, charging the modest sum of five dollars for the operation, which was quite enough to procure him a new hat. We bought oranges of the natives, there being a grove near the bank. After a delay of about twelve hours, the boats arrived and we proceeded to within a few miles of Gargano, and walked the rest of the way.

At one place in the middle of the river there was a schooner fast in the mud; the masts had been removed and it had been transformed into a hotel; we took breakfast there.

Arriving at Gargano late in the afternoon, we staid here over night. We paid a dollar for sleeping in a shed on the ground. Every building in the place was occupied. Next morning we started on foot for the City of Panama, a distance of twenty miles, arriving there in due season, completely tired out. We passed the first night in a hotel outside the city. A high wall surrounds the town, and at night the gates are closed and no one is allowed to enter.

In the morning we entered the city, and registered at a large hotel. All the public houses were crowded; not only were the beds full, but the floors were covered with men bound for California. We were sleeping on the floor one night when my brother was taken very sick. He asked me to get him some brandy and water as soon as possible. I made my way to the stairs over the sleeping men, and in my hurry I fear I stepped on some of them, for I thought my brother was dying. I was greeted with such exclamations as "Get off my toes," or "Get out of here or I'll put you out." I procured the brandy without any other mishap, and after giving it to my brother, I was greatly relieved to see him improve rapidly. He had been taken with a sudden attack of the Panama fever. The fever troubled him while he was in California, and for a number of years after he returned home. I ought to state that the City of Panama is situated on the Pacific coast. We were four days on the Isthmus. The railroad was not built at this time, but the work of construction was being pushed. There was nothing but rough roads and mule paths across the Isthmus, except a fair road several miles out of Panama, paved with cobble stones. Everything was carried across the Isthmus on pack mules or horses. We saw a pack train of thirty or forty mules and horses loaded with silver bars, which were three or four feet in length, and about three inches in thickness. The train was guarded by twenty or thirty native soldiers, armed with muskets. The silver came from some of the South American countries, Chili, Peru or Bolivia, and was being transported across the Isthmus to Chagres, to be shipped to New York or some foreign country.

The roads were very poor most of the way. It was the rainy season and everything was covered with mud. Sometimes the mules sank to their bellies in the mud. Very likely the travelling was much better in the dry season.

The Isthmus was once in the possession of brigands, whose seaports were the City of Panama and Chagres. They had armed vessels that roamed the sea on both sides of the Isthmus, and captured everything they came in contact with, making slaves of the officers, sailors and passengers. We saw quite a number of miles of road out from Panama paved with small stones by their prisoners. At last their vessels and seaports were captured by civilized nations, and the pirate kingdom was swept from the face of the earth.

There were some well dressed Spaniards and others who rode about in carriages with their families.

The country was very uneven and hilly in the interior, so much so that I have always been of the opinion that a canal could never be constructed across the Isthmus.

We spent one Sunday in the City of Panama. In the forenoon the military paraded the streets. There were also religious services in the cathedrals. In the afternoon cockfights in the streets appeared to be the principal occupation. The priests looked on to see the sport with the rest of the inhabitants. Sunday seemed to be a regular holiday. I went into one of the cathedrals where mass was being celebrated in Spanish or some other foreign tongue. There were many gold and silver images and candlesticks about the altar.

The principal streets of Panama were paved with cobble stones. Most of the buildings were two stories in height, with tiled roof. Parrots and vultures were quite plenty in and about the city. The former were numerous about the buildings and hotels. They were quite tame. They were wild in the country, which is their native place. It was against the law to kill a vulture. They are black and look like a crow, but much larger. They act as scavengers in the city. They were very numerous in the cities of Mexico where we stopped.

Soon after arriving in Panama we went to the steamship company's office to learn when we were to sail to San Francisco. There was a steamer in the harbor, ready to sail, but not the one we were booked for. But we were told at the office that we could go on that one if we would take deck passage,—a thing which we concluded to do, since we were very glad to leave such an unsettled place.

While we were on the Isthmus we found the weather mild and damp. Oranges and other fruit grow on the trees all the year round. On our way up from Panama to San Francisco we had the company of George Stevens, from Littleton, and of two brothers by the name of Stewart. They were formerly butchers in Littleton, and I was told later that they went into the same business in San Francisco.

We stopped at Acapulco twelve hours to leave the mails, and to procure some stores for the ship. Some of the passengers went on shore in the boats, Theodore and I among the rest. We had a good dinner of ham, eggs, chicken, bread and coffee, which was a great treat, after living so long on wormy bread, poor beef, fish, stale bread and poor coffee. While we were anchored in the harbor, the natives came out to the steamer in their boats, loaded with tropical fruits, which they sold to the passengers. They also had some very pretty shells, which they sold at a low price. Little boys came out to the steamer in boats. The passengers amused themselves by throwing ten-cent pieces into the water for these little fellows to dive for. Sometimes three or four were after the same piece of money. Very often the money would go down fifteen or twenty feet in the water, but they always got it, and held it up for us to see, grinning from ear to ear. It was great sport for the passengers.

When we came out of the harbor the steamer passed quite close to land, so that we could almost throw a stone to the shore. The sea was very calm on the Pacific most of the time. We saw numbers of whales, porpoises, flying fish, etc. We sailed quite near a whale ship, which signaled for our steamer to stop. A number of the whalemen came on board our steamer. They brought a large sea turtle with them, which they gave to the captain. The captain in turn gave them the New York papers and several bottles of wine. After they had been on board our steamer an hour or so, the captain asked them to leave, as he was anxious to proceed on the voyage. So eager were they to talk about home and to hear the news that the captain had to speak to them several times before they would go. They had been away from home eighteen months.

One morning we saw something that looked like men on a raft making signals to us by waving their hats or coats, as we supposed, to draw our attention. The captain thinking some one was wrecked, stopped the ship, and was on the point of sending a boat, when a great vulture flew away from what proved to be the carcass of a dead horse or cow. The passengers laughed at the captain for making such a ridiculous mistake.

Most of the way from Panama to San Francisco we were in sight of the shore. We stopped at San Diego to leave and get the mails. This was our last stopping place before arriving at San Francisco. At San Diego we ran across a man who was sick and out of money. He had taken passage from New York to California by way of Cape Horn, and for some reason had been left at San Diego. Some of the passengers asked the captain what he would take the man to San Francisco for. The sum was quite reasonable. The hat was passed among the passengers and money enough was soon raised to pay his fare to San Francisco, and have something left when he arrived. The man felt very thankful to us for helping him.

We landed in San Francisco all right, but not so strong as when we left home. We passed through the Golden Gate for the first time. The entrance to the harbor was quite narrow On the right hand side was a high bluff, but the other side was much lower. Soon after passing through the Golden Gate we came in sight of an island, Angel Island, I think it was. A fort had been built on it to defend the entrance to the harbor. After passing the island the steamer turned to the right, and the City of San Francisco was in sight. Back of the city are high hills, and part of the city is built on these hills. Looking across the bay to the north we could see Oakland, fifteen miles distant.

To the left of Oakland was the entrance to the Sacramento River. Looking down the harbor we could not see land. It looked like the ocean, so great was the distance. This is the largest and best harbor in the world.

We stopped in San Francisco a few hours, and then started for the mines, intending to go to the City of Nevada, in Nevada County, as we had read in the papers that it was a good mining locality. As we left the hotel, valises in hand, we saw Mr. Stevens in the smoking-room, smoking a cigar. He asked us where we were going, we told him to the mines. He wanted to know why we were in such a hurry, and we told him we were in no hurry, but saw no reason for stopping there. We did not see him again while we were in California.

We took the steamboat to Sacramento City, passing across the bay to the Sacramento River. As we went along we saw large numbers of wild ducks and geese. The river was very crooked, and the country on both sides of the river was very flat. The lower part of the valley is covered with a kind of reed, five or six feet in height. Further up the valley large quantities of wheat are raised.

At Sacramento we took another small steamer to Marysville, on our way to Nevada City. At Marysville my brother sent a letter home to mother. We arrived at Marysville at night, intending to start for Nevada City in the morning by stage. But the fare was so high that we concluded to walk. As we passed along the road we saw the farmers ploughing the land to put in the wheat. It was now the 12th of February.

The land was quite level for twenty-five miles on each side of the Sacramento River. We could see the mountains in the distance where the mines were situated. It was quite easy travelling till we arrived at the foot hills of the Sierra Nevada mountains. The only town we passed through was Rough and Ready, about five miles from Grass Valley, and ten miles from Nevada City. There were ranches on the road, where travellers could secure lodgings. Saturday afternoon about five o'clock we arrived at Grass Valley, situated about four miles from Nevada City. A hotel runner came to us, and wanted us to take supper at his hotel, which we did. We were very tired, travelling all day afoot. It was the custom in the mining towns at that time for the hotels to send out men to invite strangers to stop at their hotel. A great number of miners were travelling about the country prospecting for gold to find a good place to locate.

## CHAPTER II.

#### FIRST EXPERIENCES IN MINING.

After we had finished supper on the first day of our arrival in Grass Valley, the proprietor of the hotel urged us to stay there instead of going to Nevada, claiming it was a much better mining locality. There was plenty of work by the month and day to be obtained at the numerous saw mills and quartz mills of the place. Of course the landlord of the hotel expected us to board with him. He said so much, and gave such a flattering account of the place that we concluded to stay. He charged ten dollars a week for board and lodging. Quite a large number of men had walked up with us from Marysville and stopped in Grass Valley. Some had come on the same steamer with us from New York,—one man from Lowell, Mass. We had good board at the hotel, but the sleeping accommodations were rather poor, consisting of bunks, one above the other. There were but few families in the place when we arrived, the population being made up mostly of miners. In the evening the village was filled with miners, who came to, make purchases at the stores, most of them boarding themselves. Most of the miners wore course woolen suits; some of them had big breast pins of gold in their dirty shirt fronts, and large gold watches and chains.

One of our partners left for home with $16,000 in gold,

which he had obtained from the mines. He always wore a gray woolen shirt. I never knew him to board out at any of the hotels or boarding-houses of the town. We made Grass Valley our home all the time we were in California.

The next Monday morning after our arrival I started out to see the place. I went to the lower end of the village and saw a man at work alone, mining in what was called Boston ravine. He was throwing the pay dirt into the sluice with a shovel. The water washed the dirt out of the boxes and left the gold. I struck up a bargain with this man to work the rest of the day for three dollars. He told me the wages for a whole day's work were six dollars. I threw off my coat, and began to work about ten o'clock. At night he paid me, but didn't want me any longer. I was not strong, for I had had such poor living so long on the steamer that I could not do much work. My stock of money was nearly exhausted, and I was far from home; so I was naturally anxious to get to work as soon as possible. I had sixty dollars and my brother about two hundred when we first came to Grass Valley. After finishing work, I went back to the hotel and told my brother I had earned three dollars. He said I had done quite an extensive business for the first day.

Grass Valley is situated about forty miles from Sacramento in the foot hills of the Sierra Nevada Mountains, about half way between Rough and Ready and Nevada City, which are about ten miles apart. Most of the town is on the hillside overlooking the valley which is on the north. Wolf Creek runs south through the valley to the right of

FIRST EXPERIENCE IN MINING. 33

the town. Grass Valley ravine runs down from the west and enters Wolf Creek at the foot of the village. Woodpecker ravine runs into Wolf Creek from the east, about half a mile above the village. There is a flat in front of the town, called Pike Flat. All these places can be seen from the town of Grass Valley, which has a beautiful situation. About a mile south of Grass Valley on Wolf Creek is another village called Boston Ravine. When we first came to the town, most of the buildings were covered with shingles, three feet in length. For partitions between the rooms cotton cloth was used. More substantial buildings were afterwards put up of brick and lumber. Many log cabins were put up by the miners, and many of the stores were made of logs. Gambling and drinking saloons were very numerous, open all day and late in the night, Sundays and all. Three or four musicians were employed in the larger saloons to entice in strangers. I think there was but one church in the place when we arrived there in February, 1852, the Methodist South. Other churches were afterwards erected. The Methodist North, Orthodox, Episcopal, and later the Catholic church. Many of the miners and business men went or sent home for their families; society soon improved; places of business were closed on Sunday, and the saloons and gambling hells greatly reduced. There were tall pine trees and stumps two feet in height in the streets when we first came into the place. One night the wind blew very hard, blowing down one of the trees upon a dwelling-house when people were sleeping. Fortunately no one was hurt. Next morning, the citizens with axes and ropes, cut and pulled down every tree there was in the streets.

After boarding at the hotel two or three weeks, we went into a deserted log cabin and boarded ourselves for four or five dollars a week. Next we bought a "tom" pick and shovel and tried to get some gold out of the ground. I think we made about fifty cents the first day. We made up our minds it would be more profitable to work out by the month or day, until we got used to the business of mining. What we had spent at the hotel for board and for our mining tools, cooking utensils, etc., had made a big hole in our money, and we had to do something to earn some money at once.

My brother, Theodore, hired out hauling logs with a pair of oxen to William Bennett, who had a saw mill in the place. His wages were seventy-five dollars a month and board. I hired out to a man by the name of Allison to split cedar rails. I did not make much headway splitting rails, as I was still weak from my sea voyage. Shortly after I had commenced splitting rails, I heard of a new quartz mining company that was going to work on Osborne hill, situated about four miles east of Grass Valley. I engaged to go to work for them at one hundred dollars a month and board. After I had been at work for the new company a short time, my brother wanted me to secure a place for him to work in the new company, also. He did not like to work for seventy-five dollars a month, while I was getting a hundred. I told the overseer that I had a brother who would like to get

## FIRST EXPERIENCE IN MINING.

employment. He said he would let me know when there was a vacancy. Soon after there was a vacancy, and Theodore left his place hauling logs, and went to work for the company on Osborne hill, and we were together again. Our work was not hard. Sometimes we were drawing the gold bearing rock out of the ground with a windlass, sometimes hauling the rock to the mill with a mule and cart to be crushed. One day I was driving the mule with a load of quartz rock down a steep hill. The road was very narrow. On the right hand side was a steep ravine. The mule went a little too far to the right, and before I was aware of it over she went, cart and all, down into the ravine, and landed ten or twelve feet below. I thought I had killed the mule sure, and gazed down, in deep suspense, to where she was. Imagine my surprise to see her quietly eating brush. The accident happened in sight of the mill. The overseer saw me, and calling a number of the mill hands, came and helped me get the mule and cart out of the ravine. The harness was somewhat broken, but this was all the damage done. The harness and big saddle probably saved the mule from being hurt. It took some time to get the mule and cart back again into the road. The overseer thought I was rather careless, and I thought so, too. I looked out for my mule after that, when going down a steep hill. The overseer said he laughed when he saw the mule and cart go tumbling into the ravine.

After we had worked for the new company a few months, the company cut the wages down to eighty dollars a month. The drifters' wages were reduced from six to five dollars a day. Most of the men left except the drifters, we among the rest. We next went to work for Conway & Co., on Massachusetts hill, for eighty dollars a month. We afterwards went back to the Osborne Company at the reduced wages. My brother Theodore and myself, let this company have one thousand dollars at three per cent. a month. When we wanted the money we were paid promptly, though we were told that the company would have liked it longer at the same rate. The company was doubtless good, but we thought we had better send the money home, so as to have a "nest egg" in case we should get short,—everything was so uncertain in California at that time. I have known honest, hard working miners to lose their money several times over. They would save several thousand dollars, and then wait for a few hundred more before starting for home. In the meantime, before that amount was secured, their little fortunes would be greatly reduced, and frequently all gone. The Adams Express Company at one time suspended payment, and many honest miners lost all. A man of my acquaintance lost two thousand dollars through this company. One of my partners by the name of Clark, was reduced a number of times. He would get most enough to give him a good start in the world, as he thought, but always wanted a few hundred more before he started for home. Before he could get the few hundred, he would lose a part of what he had. He told me he was about discouraged. He did not fool his money away. He lost some money prospecting a quartz ledge. At another time he lost money when the Adams Express

Company failed. Again he was interested in a company of twenty, that put down a shaft on Eureka slide, that cost twenty thousand dollars. They did not strike the lead; so here was another loss. He boarded himself, washed his own clothes and lived very prudently. The last time I heard of him, he had got into another unlucky speculation.

We worked for Conway & Co. on Massachusetts hill for several months at eighty dollars a month, when we were discharged. The mill stopped for repairs. It was an eighteen stamp quartz mill, situated in Boston ravine. The company owned quartz ledges on Massachusetts and Gold hills. They afterwards bought the Lafayette ledge for seventy-five thousand dollars. We then worked in the placer mines for the Day Company for five dollars a day, and boarded ourselves. It was much harder work, but the pay was better. After we had worked for the Day Company three or four weeks, the water gave out. The company said they would give us work, if we would work nights. So we worked at night and slept in the daytime, but it was not so pleasant. After a number of weeks the company had to stop work day and night for want of water. Then we had to find employment elsewhere.

At another time my brother and I worked for a man by the name of Stiles, sinking shafts. He was employed by the Empire Gold Quartz Mining Company getting out quartz by the ton on Ophir hill. We had a dollar a foot for sinking the shafts, which were about sixty feet deep. We made good wages at this work, six or seven dollars a day, but it did not last long. At another time I cut cord wood, and sold it I cut it from the tops of trees, that had been cut down for lumber. I could cut from two to three cords a day, realizing two dollars and a half a cord.

At another time I worked three weeks for a man who was getting out shingles. They were split out of sugar pine. One tree that we worked on was seven feet through, and a hundred and fifty feet high. The tree was very clear for forty or fifty feet. The sugar pine looked something like our white pine, but made much better lumber.

One day when I was at work for Wood & Company on Osborne hill, some little distance from the mill, an Indian came near where I was, and by signs let me know that he wanted my money. He had a bow and plenty of arrows. I had no money with me. I emptied my pockets. After he was convinced that I had no money, he went away. I had nothing to defend myself with but my axe.

In the winter of 1852-53, while I was at work for the Conway Mining Company, which employed some fifteen or twenty men, we had a great snowstorm. The snow was four feet deep, so as to stop the teams hauling quartz rock to the mill to be crushed and the gold extracted. Work was stopped, both in the mill and the mines. The company were owing their help twenty thousand dollars. The overseer promised to pay as soon as he could get to work again. He gave each of us a note for the amount due us. He boarded us as long as his money lasted, and when that gave out tried to borrow, but without success, as all the property was heavily mortgaged. The company had recently bought the Lafayette Gold Quartz Mine, and had mortgaged the mill and other property in settlement. The men boarded with him as long as he could furnish them with anything to eat. One night after we had had supper, consisting of a little codfish and a few small potatoes, not knowing where we should get food the next day, we all assembled in the cabin to pass away the time as best we could, telling stories and singing songs. Everyone was expected either to tell a story or to sing a song, and they told some of the most improbable stories I ever heard. Here is one:

At the time of the Revolution the English soldiers caught one of our spies. He was tried by court martial and found guilty, and sentenced to be hanged. The soldiers tried to hang him, but the rope broke. They passed around his neck the largest rope they had, and that broke too, without doing him any harm. They said, "We'll fix him." They put a heavy charge of powder into one of their largest guns, rammed it down, put the spy on top in place of a ball, and fired it. About a quarter of a mile in front of the cannon was a piece of woods. The soldiers could see the trees fall from the contents of the cannon. They went into the woods to search for the remains of the poor spy. Imagine their surprise when they found him sitting on the stump of the last tree quietly picking the slivers out of his legs. They let him go after that. The above story was told by a New Jersey man.

In consequence of the deep snow, everything that man or beast could eat was very high and scarce. Flour went up to sixty dollars a barrel, and other things in proportion. Some of the boarding-houses had nothing for their boarders to eat, and they had to quit the business. Teams from Sacramento and Marysville, where everything came from, could not get into the place on account of the snow and mud. Tne mules and horses sank to their bellies in the roads. We had to leave Conway's and live as best we could. Theodore was at work for a man by the name of Cole, who kept a boarding-house in the village, and was lucky enough to have a stock of flour and other eatables on hand. I obtained board from him for twelve dollars a week. The snow drove the grizzly bears out of the mountains. One large one passed through Grass Valley. One of Conway's men saw him while teaming a load of wood. When first seen the bear was in the path coming towards him. The man had never seen a bear before and thought it was a cow. But he thought it was the funniest looking cow he had ever seen. When he met the bear it turned off to the left and went over the fence. The bear looked back to see if the man was coming after him. When the man got back to the village and told what he had seen, everyone said it was a grizzly bear, and very man in town who had a rifle or shot gun went after him. They killed the bear between Grass Valley and Rough and Ready, and sold the meat for forty cents a pound. It weighed eight hundred pounds.

Further up the mountains the snow was twenty feet deep. Men had to leave and come down to Nevada and Grass Valley on snowshoes. Food was sent to those in the mountains as soon as possible. Such quantities of snow had never been seen before. We managed to live through the winter without any great suffering, although some were "short" for a while. I did not hear of anyone dying of hunger. The mills all stopped work, and very little business of any kind was done. The snow did not last long, and after a few weeks everything was plenty again. In the spring the mills started up, and work was plenty again. I received my money of Mr. Conway, three hundred dollars, soon after he commenced work, though the first time I called upon him I failed to get it.

The first flour to reach Grass Valley, after the great snowstorm, was brought on pack mules by the baker. The freight on the first load of flour and provisions amounted to six hundred dollars. It was a very large load, drawn by six yoke of oxen.

At one time I worked getting out lumber for large quartz and saw mills. Sometimes we didn't work longer than two or three weeks in the same place. The mills would stop work for repairs, water would give out, or something else would happen to prevent us from working continuously in one place. All kinds of business were very uncertain, as is apt to be the case in a new country. We were at work most of the time, however, doing something.

One evening, during the period Theodore and I were at work on Osborne hill for Wood & Company at one hundred dollars per month, we went with the rest of the help to see an Indian fandango or dance, about five miles from the mill. In the woods, near the place of meeting, we saw Indians hiding behind trees, armed with bows and arrows. Sometimes some of the white men abused their women, and so they were on the lookout. We kept together so as not to get into any trouble with them. Some of our men had pistols, so that we could defend ourselves if need be, but we had no trouble with them.

The place was lighted up by a number of wood fires. There was a large wigwam, in the centre of the place, made of poles, sticks and mud, I should think. In fact, I could hardly tell what it was made of. There was but one entrance to the building, which was only about two feet high. I had to crawl on my hands and knees to get into the building. An Indian stood at the entrance, and I asked him the price of admission, for I wanted to see what was going on inside. He said three dollars. I told him I would not give so much. He then said two dollars. I told him I would not give two dollars. He said one dollar, and upon my refusing to give this sum, finally dropped to fifty cents, which I paid.

There was a large fire in the centre of the building, and the smoke went out of a hole in the roof. Ten or twelve "buck" or male Indians were dancing round the fire almost naked. They made the ground tremble with their dancing. They had some sort of music, or noise I ought to call it, but it was on the other side of the fire, and I could not see what it was composed of. There were about one hundred and fifty inside, mostly women. The squaws had some acorn soup in a bowl, which they ate with their hands. They motioned for me to eat some of it, but I told them I had been to supper. They laughed at me because I would not eat with them. They were a filthy set. There was such a foul smell in the place that I did not stop long. The squaws also had acorn soup outside the wigwam, of which we were invited to partake. I do not think many of our party accepted their invitation. We staid about two hours and then left, well satisfied with our visit. The Indians came into town quite often to get flour, and occasionally a poor piece of meat. The squaws usually came with them, with their little ones strapped to their backs. The Indians made the squaws carry all things purchased. One day I saw an Indian go by the cabin not carrying anything, while his squaw was loaded down with a pappoose and sack of flour. I asked the Indian why he didn't carry the flour. He laughed and said in Choctaw dialect, "Very good woman." I told him he was a lazy, good-for-nothing Indian. His only response was a grin. Sometimes they worked, but not very often. An Indian boy worked in a stable in Grass Valley, another worked in an eating-house at Montezuma, a small mining town on the other side of the South Yuba.

The United States government sent the Indians to a reservation away from the mining towns. They came back to Grass Valley every year to mourn for departed friends who had gone to the happy hunting grounds. Once I went to one of their places of mourning. They made a great deal of noise, hallooing and crying. I could see tears in their eyes. The chief of the Grass Valley, Wenmer, told me that he and his Indians did not like to live away from Grass Valley. He used to come to our cabin to get something to eat, which we gave him. He would thrust his head into the window or door, grin and say, "Bread, Injun muchee hungry, very good American."

We used to get a small stick of wood, four or five feet in length, split one end a little, put a twenty-five cent piece into the crack, set it upright in the ground about a hundred feet away, and let them shoot at the money with their bows and arrows. If they hit the coin they had it. On one occasion an Indian shot his arrow at the coin a number of times and failed to hit it. He then went and pocketed the piece of money, which was against the rules, but we let him have it, as everyone laughed at him because he could not hit the coin. They preferred to get money that way, rather than to work for it.

Sometimes they would steal gold from the sluice boxes while we were at dinner. One day a miner saw an Indian stealing gold from a sluice box. A number of miners chased him, but he was a better runner than any of them, and got away.

The Yuba River tribe had a fight with the Grass Valley tribe one day, and two or three were wounded on each side. That was all the battle amounted to. They were too lazy to fight. My brothers, Sherman and Edward, said they were inferior to the Indians they saw on the plains.

## CHAPTER III.

#### DESCRIPTION OF THE MINES.

The placer mines of Grass Valley extended from the surface to a depth of two hundred and twenty-five feet. Eureka slide, situated beyond the head of Grass Valley ravine, was two hundred and twenty-five feet deep. The pay dirt, or lead, of this mine was about fifty feet wide, and from six inches to two or three feet deep, and was very rich. It was a continuation of Grass Valley slide. My brother Theodore worked drifting in Grass Valley slide a short time for one of the owners, John McCoy, who was sick, for which he received seven dollars a day. It was a wet, disagreeable place to work. Drifting consists of digging out a passage in the earth, usually between shaft and shaft, following along the lead and taking out the pay dirt.

The gold is found near the bed rock, but not below it. The pay dirt usually consists of gravel from a few inches to two or three feet in depth. In the creek and ravines, where the miners first commenced to work, the poorest dirt on top was thrown to one side. Later, when labor was not so high, all this dirt was worked through the sluice boxes.

A sluice box is made of three boards, each twelve feet long, one foot wide and one inch thick, nailed together. The bottom board is made two inches narrower at one end, in order that the small end of one box will fit the large end of another box. A piece of board, two inches wide, is nailed on the bottom and top of the box at both ends and in the middle, to make the box strong enough to hold a man. Three or four pieces of board, an inch wide, are driven inside the big end of the box, four inches from the end, two inches apart to prevent the gold from leaving the box. A run of sluices is composed of twenty or more boxes, one after the other. The longer the run the more gold will be saved. One end of the box is raised two, three, four and sometimes six inches higher than the other end, thereby making one end of a long run several feet higher than the other. The boxes are usually on two stakes, one on each side, nailed together by a piece of board about a foot wide. The boxes must be perfectly tight, so that the water, gold and quicksilver can not get out. A piece of cotton cloth two inches wide is put around the small end of the box before it is put into the large end to prevent its leaking. If it leaks after that, it is calked with cotton cloth. The water is let into the upper box, and goes down through the whole run of boxes. The pay dirt is put into the boxes with a shovel. The water washes the dirt and gravel out. If there are any large stones that the water will not carry out of the box, a man walking on top of the boxes, throws them out with a long-handled fork.

The gold being very heavy, settles down into the bottom of the box, and is prevented from escaping by pieces of boards fastened in the big end of the box. When the gold is taken out, a small quantity of water is run down through the boxes. The pieces of board, above mentioned, are taken out, and quicksilver is sprinkled by means of a soda bottle with a cotton rag tied over the end. The amalgam is swept out of the boxes at the end of the run with a small broom into an iron pan, water is put into the pan, then the pan is shaken over a hole, and the sand and all other impurities are washed out. This process is called "panning out." The amalgam is then strained through a buckskin bag, made for that purpose. It is then put into an iron pan and put over a hot fire, where the mercury is burnt off. A magnet is then used to take out any particles of iron. The gold is then boiled five or ten minutes in nitric acid, washed and dried, and is then ready to be sold. Our company at first used to hire the druggist at the village to clean the gold, but later we bought a magnet and nitric acid, and cleaned it ourselves. Most of the deep diggings were discovered after the cracks and ravines were worked out. The dirt and gravel in the cracks and ravines was a foot to five or six feet in depth, down to the bed work.

Wolf Creek, Boston Ravine, and Grass Valley ravine were rich. Woodpecker ravine paid well, but not so well as the others I have mentioned. Pike Flat, through which Wolf Creek runs opposite Grass Valley to the north, had a very rich lead, which extended about half way the length of Pike Flat, and then turning to the left, run out in the old Point and Day diggings at the edge of the flat and on the hill. The Day Company found a specimen of clear gold worth five hundred dollars. The Flat was about twelve feet deep down to the bed rock. The lead was from six inches to two feet deep, and thirty or forty feet wide. The

Day and Point diggings paid well, the latter more regularly than any other diggings I ever worked in. The trouble with these mines was that they did not last long. None of them lasted longer than five or six years, and many not so long as that.

The miners ran a ditch and tunnel into Pike flat to drain the mines, as it was very wet. We on the point were troubled somewhat with water, but little, however, as our claims did not extend far into the flat. We had a flume at the end of our runs into which the "tailings" ran. We cleaned out this flume once in three or four weeks, and even then did not save all the gold, for some would run away with the dirt. Nothing was ever invented capable of saving all the gold. It was fine as flour. We never found any pieces of gold at the point larger than two or three dollars. The Day Company ran their "tailings" into a ditch which had never been cleaned out.

No one knew how much gold was in the ditch, but the Company offered the gold for sale for fifteen hundred dollars, but no one would take it; so it was cleaned out by them selves, and they realized $10,000. The expense of cleaning the ditch was not more than one hundred dollars. What a little fortune for us, if we had only known the amount of gold in the ditch.

At another time a man named Bosworth offered us claims for three hundred dollars, which afterwards proved to be very rich. He went to the states, and returned with his wife and wife's sister, and is now postmaster of Grass Valley, or was in 1886, when I was last there.

The deep mines of Grass Valley, except quartz mines, were Grass Valley slide and Eureka slide. The latter was two hundred and twenty-five feet deep, and was worked for many years. An engine was used to pump out the water, and hoist out the dirt.

The quartz mines were extensive, and lasted longer than the placer mines; but the working was more expensive. They were mostly in the hills. Grass Valley was said to have the richest quartz mines in the world. The Allison ranch gold quartz ledge was the richest ever discovered.

Some of the quartz mines worked in 1859, were still yielding gold when I was last there in 1886. Massachusetts hill was very rich in quartz bearing rock.

It was situated a mile from Grass Valley on the south side of Boston Ravine. A little to the north of Massachusetts hill is Gold hill, which had a rich quartz ledge. Men made sixteen dollars a day crushing the croppings of the ledge with a hand mortar, when the ledge was first discovered.

An Englishman sold a claim eighty feet square for five thousand dollars. We could see gold in nearly every bucketful taken from the earth. There was a good ledge on Church hill, this side of Gold hill, near the village of Grass Valley. I heard that each of the company made $75,000 clear of expense. Lafayette ledge was being worked when I was there in 1886.

The Empire Company had a quartz mill on Wolf Creek, near Boston Ravine. They had a good ledge on Ophir hill, about one mile east of Grass Valley. They afterwards moved their mill on to the hill, so as to be near the ledge. Work was going on at this mill in 1886.

There was another quartz ledge on Osborne hill, about four miles northeast of Grass Valley, owned by Wood & Co., where my brother and I worked for a while when we first came to Grass Valley. A mill was put up in the ravine near the hill. It ran for a while and then stopped. I never heard of its starting up again. I am inclined to think the mine did not pay.

A large twenty-four stamp mill was put up near Union hill, situated about one mile north of Grass Valley, which ran for a while, and then stopped, and I think never started up again. When I was there in 1886, I found it difficult to find the place where the mill used to stand. The ledge was four feet thick. Gold could be seen in the rock. When the company quit work they could not pay their help. We lost three hundred dollars by them. One of the company offered us his gold watch and chain, which we refused to take, as we wanted the money. We never obtained anything for our work.

I suppose there are other quartz ledges near Grass Valley that I have not described; new ones are being discovered nearly every year. A company that had some rich claims on Gold hill lost the lead. They told their men that if they found it again they would give them a thousand dollars. The company kept the men at work and found it again, richer than ever.

An Englishman that had some rich claims on Massachusetts hill, lost the lead, or the ledge did not pay, and could not pay his bills. He was very proud and a high liver, having wine on his table every day. His help kept dunning him for their pay. His bad luck worked on his mind so that he poisoned himself, his wife, and two children. He left a note stating that he did not see how he could pay his bills, and had made up his mind to kill himself. He thought his wife and children would be better off out of the world, than in it with no money. He and his family had many friends, and were much liked in Grass Valley. His claims afterwards paid well, and he would have been all right, if he had not got discouraged. My brother and I at one time worked prospecting for quartz rock on Osborne hill. The claim did not pay, and so the owner could not pay us. He was owing us three hundred dollars for work. My brother saw him in San Francisco on our way home, and managed to secure seventy-five dollars. The rest we had to lose. We thought the man honest, but without the money to pay.

Quartz ledges are usually found on the top of the hills, called croppings of the ledge. They descend into the hill at an angle of about forty-five degrees, more or less. The pitch of the ledge is determined, and then a shaft is sunk in front of the ledge fifty to one hundred feet, till the ledge is struck. A drift is then run at the bottom of the shaft on both sides on the line of the ledge, one hundred feet each way, and the rock is taken out to the croppings. Another shaft is then put down on the line of the ledge and worked in the same way as the first shaft. If the ledge is found to be rich at the bottom of the shaft, another line of shafts is put down in front of the first, or an inclined shaft is put in and worked in the same way. Water is usually found at the depth of one hundred feet, and the air is frequently found to be bad. An engine is used to pump out the water and to pump good air into the mine, and take out the quartz rock and pay dirt. Some ledges are worked by a tunnel, others by an inclined shaft.

There were two tunnels in Gold hill, one owned by Conway & Company, the other by the Gold Hill Mining Company, the latter an English company. The Church Hill Mining Company used an inclined shaft. A Catholic church had been built on the hill, giving the name, Church hill. The shaft was nine feet wide and three and a half feet high. The shaft had to be well timbered to prevent the earth from caving in. The shaft was commenced on top of the ground, and followed down on the ledge as far as they wish to go. A track was laid in the shaft, and the rock and waste dirt were taken out with a car. At the bottom of the shaft a turntable was constructed.

Spermaceti candles had to be used to light up the drifts. I think the Allison Ranche Gold Mining Company used an inclined shaft to work their mine. Their shaft was down one thousand feet, when I left in 1859. The company had paid $1,000,000 in dividends. One of the company told me his dividends amounted to five hundred dollars a week.

I helped prospect a quartz ledge situated in my upper claims above the point diggings, on the edge of Pike Flat. The company struck the croppings of the ledge by accident, while we were at work on the claims, washing out gold. We obtained two hundred dollars in gold out of a panful of the croppings. It was a big prospect and in a good locality, and we thought we had a big thing. An article was put into the Grass Valley paper, giving an account of our big find. An engine had to pump out the water, as it was very wet. We did not care to go to the expense of buying and running an engine, so we gave the company half the mine for the use of their engine. We put in an inclined shaft and did all the work below ground. We worked till the ledge gave out and came to solid rock the whole length of the drift. We told the company that furnished the engine, that we did not think it was of any use to work any longer, but told them we would work till they said stop. They thought as we did, and stopped work, calling it a bad job.

We took out about forty tons of gold bearing rock. It paid well, what there was of it, but not enough to pay our expenses. The company that put in the engine lost from twelve to fifteen hundred dollars. We lost in labor, tools, and the cost of putting in the shaft. There were five in the company.

Most of the ledges are not solid rock; there is usually pay dirt above and below the ledge. Most of the quartz rock can be taken out with a pick and iron bar. The large pieces usually do not weigh more than seventy-five to one hundred pounds, from that down to small pieces. Sometimes the ledge is solid, and has to be blasted. The Allison Ranche ledge ran into the solid rock after it had been worked one hundred feet, and had to be blasted. But the gold quartz rock was four or five feet, and very rich. Lafayette ledge, also, had to be blasted. The solid quartz rock sometimes is put on to cord wood; then the wood is set on fire to make it easier to crush.

The Union Quartz Mill was the largest in Grass Valley, having twenty-four stamps. The smallest mill had five stamps. One stamp weighs about twelve hundred pounds. The lower part is made of iron, which is fastened to a piece of timber six or seven feet in length, and six inches square. The stamps are worked up and down in a large iron mortar by steam power. While the quartz rock is crushed, water is run into the mortar with the quartz rock. After the rock is crushed very fine, it is run together with the gold through a fine sieve into a trough covered with woolen blankets, where some of the gold stops. What does not stop here runs down into some batteries, where quicksilver is used to gather the fine particles of gold. The batteries are set in motion by a belt from the engine, so as to cause the gold to settle to the bottom. The blankets are changed quite often.

The gold is washed off the blankets into a tub, cleaned and made ready for the market in the same way as in placer mining, only a retort is used instead of an iron pan, so as to save all the quicksilver.

A history of the Allison Mine, at this point, might prove interesting. The ledge was discovered by accident. It was named after the owner of the ranch on which it was discovered. Some miners who were working in Wolf Creek noticed the outcroppings, and thinking the rock looked rich, mined a few tons and had them crushed at the quartz mill, little thinking it was the richest ledge ever discovered. The outcroppings paid big. They mined enough to pay for putting in an eighteen stamp mill, and their fortune was made.

DESCRIPTION OF THE MINES. 55

The quartz mills in Grass Valley got fifteen dollars a ton for crushing the rock and cleaning the gold ready for market. And they were glad to do it at that price.

As I was acquainted but little in other parts of California, I have made no attempt to describe any mines except those in or near Grass Valley.

## CHAPTER IV.

#### MINING IN GRASS VALLEY.

We visited Nevada and Rough and Ready several times, when we could not work on our own claim for want of water. Nevada has always been the county seat of Nevada county.

We worked by the day and month, sunk shafts by the foot, and cut cord wood to get money to buy into some of the mining companies and to learn the business.

We made enough the first year to buy into a company, and went to work on our own claims.

While my brother was at work drifting, he was told that good paying claims could be had in the Point Mining Company. My brother decided to have an interest, and forwarded three hundred dollars to pay for it. For many months he was without the interest and the money, but finally the money was returned with interest. Both of us secured an interest in the same mine later, which proved a good investment.

The Point Mining Company claims were situated on a point running into Pike Flat, opposite Woodpecker ravine, about a quarter of a mile from Grass Valley.

The company included seven or eight men, each man having different interests; one being a quarter, another an eighth, etc. Each man was entitled to five dollars a working day. The man having the largest interest was the overseer or boss, and he hired all the men, and did all the business. After expenses were paid, the rest paid dividends. The company settled with the men every Saturday night. Most of the company lived in a log cabin near the mine, and worked with the men. One of the members of the company, Daniel Russell, lived with us. Ernest, from Texas, one of the company, who held the largest interest and was the "boss," sold out to a man by the name of Nephie, who had come from New York to California by way of Cape Horn, with Russell. Nephie then became "boss." He went home with $16,000, having worked in the claims between two and three years. I was in his cabin once, a short time before he left, and he had eight thousand dollars in gold dust in a bowl on the table. He said that was half his fortune, as he had already sent home eight thousand dollars. His home was in Newburgh, New York. Ernest, after arriving in New York, wrote to us, and stated that the heat was greater than he had ever known it in Texas. We afterwards learned that both he and Nephie arrived home safely with their little fortunes.

Daniel Russell staid in the cabin with us until the arrival of my brothers, Sherman and Edward, and was there when we left in 1853. Three of us lived in a cabin twelve feet square, for which we paid fifty dollars, and boarded ourselves. The members of the company used to visit each other frequently. The "boss's" cabin was the headquarters.

Some members of the company assisted the "boss" in cleaning and disposing of the gold. Any member of the company was at liberty to see the "boss" cleaning and disposing of the gold, and he usually invited the members who happened to be about the cabin to go with him. Gold and silver composed the money used in California at that time.

We had letters from home once a month, and sometimes oftener, and found them a great treat. The miners used to start for the village, as soon as they heard a steamer had arrived with the mail. A steamer edition of the Boston Journal we usually bought of a newsdealer in Grass Valley.

In the fall of 1853 we received a letter from my brother Sherman, stating that he and my brother Edward had arrived at Downesville, California, having made the journey across the plains. For they had heard from mother the year before, when they started, that we were in Grass Valley. Edward was sick in bed with the mountain fever. They were out of money, but said nothing to us of the fact. Sherman worked in a restaurant, until such time as Edward should be able to travel, to get money to pay doctor's bills and other expenses. They each paid thirty dollars to get across the plains, and drove cattle for their board. They walked from Downesville to Grass Valley, a distance of seventy-five miles.

One night as I was coming up from the claim with a pail of water to get supper, I met Sherman looking for us. If two men were glad to see one another, we were. We went down to the village and found Edward. They had separated in order to find us the more readily.

After we had all arrived at the cabin, Theodore suggested that we get supper at the best hotel in the village. No, they only wanted potatoes and salt. We got them a good supper, but they did not eat much besides potatoes and salt, nor did they eat anything else for a week. They had been without potatoes and vegetables all summer, and it seemed impossible for them to get enough.

We sat up till late in the night, talking about friends at home, their journey across the plains, and our prospects in California, and we kept it up for a week.

Brother Sherman lacked a few months of being twenty years old. Edward was two years younger. After their arrival they lived with us for a time, Russell going to another cabin. Four men living in a cabin twelve feet square and boarding themselves. What would the people in old Massachusetts think of such doings? Many of the miners who had plenty of money were living in the same way.

For quite a number of years before and after my brothers crossed the plains, large numbers of cattle and horses were purchased in Missouri and the adjoining states, and driven across the plains to California. Cattle could be bought in Missouri for ten dollars a head, that would bring over one hundred dollars in California. Horses that cost only thirty or forty dollars, after being driven across the plains, sold for two hundred dollars. Many emigrants brought their families in covered wagons, drawn by four and six yoke of oxen. They cooked their own food outside the wagons, and stopped at night to sleep. They averaged only eight or ten miles a day, and even then the feet of the cattle frequently became so sore that they had to be covered with buffalo hide. It was a rough journey, and many cattle and horses died on the way. But much money was made in the business. The building of the Pacific Railroad put a stop to this kind of traffic.

When Sherman and Edward had been with us about a week, Sherman said, "Ed., I guess we had better start for the southern mines. We've been here long enough." Wild as two hawks! With some difficulty we persuaded them to stay with us, for we were convinced that mining in the south was no more profitable than at Grass Valley.

One evening, some days later, as we were walking down town to hear some speaking by different candidates for county officers, Sherman called my attention to a tall well-dressed man, whom he said he thought he knew. I advised him not to speak to the man, for fear he might be mistaken.

As the speakers, one after another, were presented to the audience, this man was introduced as Wm. M. Stewart, of Nevada City, candidate for district attorney for Nevada county. After the speaking was over, Sherman made his way to Mr. Stewart, and asked him if he was not a graduate of Yale. Mr. Stewart said, "Yes." My brother said he was Fletcher, Yale '52. Stewart said that Sherman had changed so much since he had last seen him, that he did not know him. And that was not strange, for Sherman had on an old blouse he had worn across the plains, and was very thin in flesh. They had a long talk that evening. Sherman did not get back to the cabin till after midnight. This Stewart is now United States Senator from the state of Nevada, serving his third term.

Stewart invited Sherman to come to Nevada City and

make him a visit. He also offered him the privilege of studying law with him, using his office, books, etc. We told Sherman he had better go, and gave him two twenty dollar gold pieces. He went down town, bought a new suit of clothes, had his hair cut, and his beard taken off, and looked like a different man. He visited Stewart, and after returning to Grass Valley, was eager to begin the study of law at once. We advised him to do so, since he was fitted by education for just that kind of business. We agreed to furnish him with all the money he needed, which he could pay back when he was ready. We gave him fifty dollars and he started for Nevada. We did not see him again for a week. The prominent lawyers in Nevada seemed to like him, and gave him the opportunity to take evidence in court, collect doubtful bills, etc. In this way he picked up considerable money, but not enough to pay his bills. We gave him money whenever he called for it.

One Sunday after he had begun the study of law, he came to visit us. We noticed he had lost flesh, and did not look as well as usual. We asked him if he was well. He said, "Yes." But we found out that he had been living in a log cabin with some miners, so as not to spend so much money for board. We advised him to board at a good hotel, and told him he would soon have money enough. And so it proved, for the following winter he was appointed editor of a paper, at a salary of twenty-five dollars a week, the proprietor being lawyer Searles.

Soon after the boys arrived in Grass Valley, Theodore sold to Edward an interest in a claim at Wolf Creek for one hundred and twenty-five dollars. He was to pay when he got the money. He got enough out of the claim to pay for it, and then sold it for what he gave. He then went to work by the day. The claim was situated some distance from the cabin, and besides he wanted to live near his work. The claim, too, would soon be worked out.

We still worked on the Point claims, which paid well. One time, when we were cleaning up for the day, the Orthodox minister made us a visit, and seeing we had a good quantity of gold for our day's work, asked us for a subscription to aid him in building a new church. He was then preaching in a hall over the drug store in town. Two of us subscribed five dollars each. The "boss," and those who did not subscribe anything, made lots of fun of us for "giving to the priest." Later we found the "boss" had given twenty-five dollars to build the Methodist South, and we had a laugh on him, too.

For two days, July 3 and 4, a fair was held to help the Orthodox church. The building was put up and boarded, but they did not have money enough to finish the inside. The ladies took hold of the work, and we all had a good time. Fifteen hundred dollars was cleared. Brother Theodore and I went in the evenings and spent twenty-five or thirty dollars each. The last night of the fair all articles not sold were disposed of at auction. Many of the mill owners and business men of the town were there to help the church. For the stronger the church, the weaker the power of the gambling hells and saloons would be. The mill owners would bid against one another at the auction on articles worth only a few dollars, and run them up sometimes as high as fifty dollars. They did not care for the money as long as it went for the church. There was a good deal of sport at the auction. There was a large attendance at the fair both evenings.

During my second visit to California I was present at another fair, gotten up for the benefit of the Episcopal church. The fair was held in an unfinished schoolhouse. The admission was five dollars. The ladies furnished the supper free, of course. They began dancing before supper, and so offended the minister that he left. Lawyer Dibble took charge of the arrangements afterwards, and everybody had a good time. A large sum of money was realized, as the party was well attended. That was the last dancing party I ever attended, taking an active part. The loss of my leg put a stop to my dancing arrangements.

This same minister, who showed his bad temper by leaving the party, afterwards took an equally abrupt departure from town at the point of the pistol. A storekeeper in the village accused him of making too frequent calls on his wife. Finally things came to a crisis, and the unfortunate minister was seen running from Grass Valley, chased by the irate storekeeper, pistol in hand. He was lost sight of at Marysville, however. It is safe to say that he never showed his head again at Grass Valley.

## CHAPTER V.

DEPARTURE FOR HOME.

Late in the fall of 1853, my brother Theodore and I thought of going home. We sold our interests in the Point claims about December 10, 1853, for what they had cost us, after working them for a year. We gave Sherman what money he thought he should need. He gave his note, which he paid when he got the money a year or two later. Edward decided to stay and work in the mines. He continued to live in our cabin.

We bade good bye to our brothers, partners and friends, and started for home about the middle of December. Theodore never saw Sherman again. We took the stage for Sacramento at twelve o'clock at night. Edward and Sherman saw us off. We had our gold in buckskin bags in a valise. We arrived at San Francisco with our gold all right, at ten o'clock the next night.

On our journey to Sacramento and later on the boat, I noticed a man who seemed to be staring at me every time I looked at him. Theodore noticed it also. We concluded he was one of those fellows, only too numerous in California, who would take our gold from us if he had a good chance. Arriving in San Francisco, we landed our gold in the express office as soon as possible. Here, too, we saw the same man who stared at us so much on the journey.

He, too, deposited his gold dust. He was a miner, just out of the mines. We had a talk with him later. We found he had been just as suspicious of us as we had been of him. We all three of us had a great scare for nothing.

Upon depositing our gold dust at the Adams Express office, we were told that it would cost three per cent. to send it home, but if we would give the company the use of it until the first of May, the express charges would be nothing at all. We concluded to do the latter, and obtained the money all right the first of May. There were three steamers going out of San Francisco on the same day, with passengers and freight for New York, all in opposition to one another, two by way of Panama, and one by the Nicaragua route. We bought second cabin tickets by Nicaragua for ninety dollars through to New York. I heard afterwards that steerage tickets were sold for twenty-five dollars each, an hour before the steamers sailed. This was quite a reduction from the cost of a ticket going out, for we had paid one hundred and eighty dollars each for much inferior accommodations. I was informed that the steamship companies paid twenty-five dollars for transporting each passenger across the Isthmus of Panama by rail, for the Panama railway had just been completed.

Opposition is the life of trade, and travel, too. There was some betting among the passengers as to which line would be the first to reach New York. Our steamer had a hot box, a few days out from San Francisco. The crew had to pump water from the ocean to cool it.

Off the Gulf of Tehuantepec we encountered a severe

storm. One of the passengers who had never been to sea before, having crossed the plains in going to California, thought the ship had struck a rock. So scared was he that he ran up on deck in his night clothes, intending to jump overboard. The ship was in no danger, and the unfortunate man was laughed at not a little by the passengers the next morning, for getting so excited for nothing.

A few days before we arrived at the Isthmus we could see the fire coming out of the mountains at night. It was volcanoes. Nothing else of importance occurred on our voyage to Juan del Sur. The steamer anchored about half a mile from the town. There were no wharves. The passengers were taken in rowboats as far as the boats could go, and then carried to dry land on the backs of the natives, so that we did not wet our feet, though it was rather a disagreeable way of travelling, especially for the ladies, of whom there were quite a number. There were hundreds of the natives on shore, with mules saddled and bridled, ready to take us across to the lake. The distance was only twelve miles.

We landed about ten o'clock in the morning, and before starting for the lake I purchased a breakfast, consisting of bread, ham, coffee and eggs, mostly eggs. I never saw such a place for eggs. They were peddled about the streets the same as oranges or other fruit, boiled harder than brickbats. After dinner I picked out a good looking mule, and giving my ticket to a Spaniard, mounted. But the animal refused to go. The man gave me a switch, and by signs told me to strike the mule over the head. This I did. Away went the mule at a lively rate. Sometimes she would stop and back, but with a good application of the switch over the head, would go on again. I did not apply the switch to any other part of the mule's body to see what the effect would be. I thought it best to let well enough alone. The passengers kept together all the way to the lake. Some had hard work to make their mules go at all. Arriving at the lake I left the mule in the street, according to the orders of the man of whom I had obtained it in Juan del Sur.

There were no hills to trouble us, and the travelling was much better than at Panama; the climate, too, was very much better. We did not hear of any sickness on our way across. The best cup of chocolate I ever had, I bought of an old woman at the lake. The inhabitants had things to sell the passengers, such as tropical fruits and sea shells, as at Acapulco and other places where we stopped.

We started to go across the lake in the afternoon of the day we arrived. It was very stormy most of the night. I thought we should go to the bottom before morning.

We arrived at the mouth of the river San Juan about ten o'clock the next morning. We then took another small steamer, that was waiting for us to go down the river. At one place we had to land and walk by some rapids, below which we embarked upon another steamboat, which took us to Greytown, on the Atlantic coast. We went down some very steep rapids in the San Juan on the second boat. At night the boat was tied to a tree on the bank. Near the landing where we stopped for the night lived a negro and his wife. They had been slaves in South Carolina and bought their freedom. They provided the passengers with supper, consisting mostly of eggs, as usual, for which we paid them the modest sum of fifty cents. They did not cook fast enough, and some of the passengers assisted them. Quite a number of the passengers would be eating at one time, and when they finished another lot would come up from the boat. This was kept up all night. The negro and his wife made a good sum out of the passengers that night. Some of the passengers tried to keep the others from sleeping, and kept up a racket all night. It was taken good naturedly, but I think very few slept on the boat that night.

At daylight the next morning we started for Greytown, arriving there about the middle of the afternoon. We took our supper on shore. In fact, we always took our meals on shore when we could.

At this place the alligators were very troublesome, killing many of the natives, especially when they went into the water. Before dark we went on board the steamer, Star of the West, which was waiting for us. It was the same ship that the United States government sent to provision Fort Sumter in the spring of 1861. The steamer was anchored a mile from shore, and was reached by rowboats. She sailed sometime during the night for New York. At daylight the next morning we were nearly out of sight of land. Our living on board the Star of the West was excellent, fully as good as at any hotel I was ever in, roast turkey and beef, chicken, all kinds of fruit, and everything else that was good. We sat at the same table as first cabin passengers. Our sleeping arrangements were inferior to those of the first cabin passengers, but very good.

## DEPARTURE FOR HOME.

One stormy morning, off the Island of Cuba, we saw another steamer going in the same direction we were, supposed to be one of the opposition lines that started with us from San Francisco. The steamer went ahead of us, but was in sight two or three days. At one time we lost sight of it, but saw it again when nearing New York. We were anxious to reach New York first. Our captain said he would be in New York first, and so it proved. The captain said he knew the way to New York, as well as he knew the cow-path in his father's pasture at home.

The fireman put barrels of pork, rosin and other combustibles into the furnaces to make steam. The fire came out of the smokestack to the height of six feet. The captain stood over the pilot-house to direct the ship. Two men were at the wheel. The first mate was at the wheel, also, to make sure the orders were obeyed. The wheels went faster and faster, but without gaining on the other steamer. It seemed impossible for our boat to go any faster.

Our boat being only twelve hundred tons burden, while the other was three thousand tons, we could go straight to New York, while the other would be obliged to take a pilot, and go through a crooked channel. We reached quarantine fifteen minutes before our rival, and as they came up, all our company assembled in the after part of the boat and gave them three times three.

We made the passage from San Francisco to New York in twenty-three days, the shortest time on record up to that time.

About the eighth of January, at nine o'clock, we were in New York, glad and thankful to have a good bed for the first time in two years.

We reached Littleton on the tenth of January, and spent the rest of the winter in visiting, and talking of the wonderful gold country.

I showed a neighbor a piece of gold, and asked what he thought it was worth. He guessed about five dollars, and seemed much surprised when I said it was worth fifty dollars.

I believe we were the first men to reach Littleton who were better off than when we started, although several had gone to California. Everyone was anxious to hear of our adventures.

I stayed at home a year, and bought a farm, but finding it did not pay as well as mining, sold out.

## CHAPTER V.

### RETURN TO CALIFORNIA.

Late in the fall of 1854 I was stopping at home. My father had a chaise he wanted to sell. I started into the country, and went in the direction of Princeton and Phillipston. Not being able to sell the chaise I tried to trade it for a cow or heifer.

At night I stopped at a hotel at Templeton. I knew my father had some cousins at Templeton, named White. I enquired for them, and learned that Asa White lived near the hotel.

I called on Asa White, but not finding him in returned to the hotel. Very soon Mr. White came and invited me to spend the night at his home, which I was very glad to do. I knew him very well. He used to keep a pump and lead pipe store on Dock Square, Boston. Father used to supply his family with butter, eggs and berries from the farm. I remembered seeing him when I went to Boston with father, when a boy.

I told Mr. White my errand, and he advised me to put the chaise in his swamp in the morning, pile brush around it, and set the whole on fire. I concluded to take the chaise back to Littleton. Chaises were out of style, and were beginning to be hard to sell.

Asa White was a very hospitable man, and good company. He was a good hand to tell stories, and a great hand to speculate. I told him I intended to return to California. Mr. White said he had five thousand apple trees he would like to have me take to California. I told Mr. White I did not want to take them, as I should not know what to do with them. He appeared anxious to have me take the trees with me, and at last I consented. Mr. White was to box them up, and send them to me at Littleton. He was to have one-half the money for the trees, after deducting expenses. They were small trees, about six inches long. A small box held them all.

I tried to sell them to a nurseryman at Sacramento City, but did not have an offer for them. I sold them at Marysville for forty dollars. This just about paid expenses. That was the last of the tree speculation.

Asa White had been to California, and I think he said he had been in business in Sacramento City.

Theodore, my brother, thought I had better take some money back with me, that I might buy into some claims as soon as I arrived in Grass Valley. I sent seven hundred dollars by the Adams Express Company. No charge was made for taking the money to California, as money had to be shipped from here to pay for gold dust.

I bought a first cabin ticket, for which I paid two hundred and fifty dollars. I went by way of Panama.

When the steamer sailed from New York, there was the usual sad leave taking of friends of the passengers. Persons on board would run out to the end of the wharf to say good bye. Some were weeping; ladies waved their handkerchiefs, but we were soon out sight of land, and I was glad of it. This exhibition was confined mostly to steerage passengers.

Nothing unusual occurred during the voyage, except one death.

A day or two before arriving at Panama, a lady passenger died of consumption. Her brother was in California, and had sent for her, hoping the climate would benefit her health. When she came on board at New York she was assisted by two nurses, she was so feeble.

Her sister and friends sat opposite me at the table. One morning I noticed their seats were vacant. I inquired of a passenger the cause of their absence, and learned the invalid had died during the night. She was buried on the Isthmus. What a sad funeral, so far from home, and in a strange land!

On the Pacific side of the Isthmus we stopped at Acapulco and San Diego, in Southern California to leave the mails. I arrived in San Francisco the second time January 1, 1854.

After selling my apple trees, I went to Grass Valley, where lived my two brothers, Sherman and Edward. Sherman was district attorney for Nevada County; previously he had edited a newspaper.

I was soon at work at my old business, and bought an interest in my old claims at the same price I had sold them for the previous year.

I was lucky enough to draw all my money from the Adams Express Company three weeks before the company failed.

My brothers were interested in some claims in Shady Creek. Two shares were for sale for eight hundred dollars. We added two more partners, and bought the claims. They were in the bed of the creek and had not been much worked. We were also entitled to bank claims on the side of the creek.

My brother, being a lawyer, hired a man named George Edmunds to work in his place. This man afterwards bought Sherman's interest for five hundred dollars, and became one of the company. We were glad to have him for a partner. He was a good fellow to work, and a good fellow every way. Edmunds afterwards sold his claim for seven hundred and fifty dollars. Placer mines were getting scarce, and we thought they would be valuable in a few years, as, in fact it proved.

The claims were twelve miles west of Nevada City, near Oak Tree Ranch, between Cherokee and San Juan.

Provisions and mining tools being much cheaper at Grass Valley, we bought a two-horse load of them, and had them transported to Shady Creek.

We had worked here about a year when other parties put in a dam at the foot of our claims to take the water out of the creek to go to French corral by flume and ditch to wash some hydraulic claims situated there. To back the water on our claims would ruin them. I told my brother Sherman about the matter. He was now practising law at Nevada City, his office as district attorney having expired. He told me to tear the dam out. The water had been taken out of there before, but the dam had been abandoned for about two years. It looked like having a lawsuit on our hands. My brother advised not to have a lawsuit, if I could help it, for he said it would cost a thousand dollars at least. On the day we destroyed the dam, Charlie Cornell, who kept the Oak Tree Ranch, told me that we would all be in jail before night, for the parties who had constructed the dam were rich and powerful. I said I thought we were able to take care of ourselves. The parties who put in the dam went to Nevada for writs to arrest us. But through the influence of Stewart and McConnell, their attorneys, and my brother Sherman, the matter was compromised. The water was to be taken out a mile further up the creek in a ditch round the hill, and across my claims in a flume. I furnished two men for three weeks to assist them in their work, the other parties doing the same. Our claims were thus saved from injury, and we had no further trouble. The other parties, however, still claimed they had the right to put in the dam.

For about eight months in the year, when there was water, I worked on my claims in Grass Valley, and Edward took charge of the mines at Shady Creek. Our company got into another dispute at Shady Creek. One day, when I was at work at Grass Valley, I received a note from Edward at Shady Creek, stating that some parties living near had "jumped" one of our bank claims, and he and Nevins, one of the company, could not get them off the ground, and I was asked to come at once. I started in the afternoon of the same day, which happened to be Saturday, arriving at Shady Creek at night. Sunday we all took a walk to Cherokee. From what Edward and Nevins said I inferred that they came near having a free fight, trying to get the men off the ground. The man who "jumped" the ground was from Northern Georgia, and had friends living near by. He had said at Cherokee, that he would leave his dead body on the ground before he would give up an inch of the claim. I told my partners I did not consider a man very dangerous who would talk that way.

Monday morning after listening to all kinds of advice from my other partners, I asked George Edmunds, a big, powerful man, who I thought would come out first in a fight, if he would go up with me and help get them off. He consented. I told the others to keep out of sight, for I thought I could secure possession of the claims better without them, as they had tried their hand and failed. Edward advised me to take the pistol, for we had a good Colt's revolver in the cabin, as they were a "tough crowd." I thought best not to take it, however, and laid it on the table. George Edmunds and I took our picks and shovels and started for the disputed ground, which was about a quarter of a mile from the cabin, leaving the rest behind. They were near us when we arrived on the disputed ground, but kept behind the trees out of sight. The claim was staked off, and a notice had been put up on a tree, forbidding any one working the ground. I tore down the notice, pulled up the stakes and threw them into the creek, and told George to sink a shaft, I doing the same. I thought this would bring things to a head, and it did. Very soon the Georgian put in appearance, trembling with excitement, and wanted to know why we were at work on his claim. George and I stopped work, and listened to what he had to say. After he had got through with his story, I told him our company laid claim to a hundred feet square of the ground in dispute, that we were entitled to a bank claim, according to the laws of the district, being owners of the creek claims. We had come to Shady Creek, bought the ground, and paid our money for it. There was no use fighting, for that would not settle the dispute. He finally admitted that we were entitled to the bank claim, in front of his claim that had been worked out. The hundred feet took in all the lead, and was all we wanted. He sent for a tape line, and measuring the hundred feet square, gave up the ground. The other partners, seeing that the dispute was settled, came down to where we were, and also the Georgian's partners, of whom there were quite a number, and we had quite a crowd present before we went away. They commenced staking off the ground to our front and right, on the hill. Ed. said he would not have them staking off ground that did not belong to them. I told him there was nothing there. We had all we claimed and all the lead. I went back to Grass Valley. There was no more trouble. Edward worked the the ground afterwards. It paid sixteen dollars per man for several weeks. The claim in dispute was on a point of land running down into the creek, making a sudden turn in the creek. A lead of gold ran through it. The other party's claim went about half way across this. We claimed one hundred feet square beyond them. How did that lead get into the point of land? This was a puzzle. Gold was found hundreds of feet down in the earth; at other places, but a few feet from the surface; sometimes there was no lead, but all the dirt paid, from the top down to the bed-rock. There was no rule about finding these leads. Miners had to hunt for them with pick and shovel and pan. Sometimes rich leads were discovered by accident. Some rivers, creeks and ravines were very rich, others not worth working.

We worked on our claims at Shady Creek for two years, and then sold out for eight hundred dollars each, which was four or five times as much as we paid. One of the partners sold his share later for one thousand dollars. About a week or ten days after we had sold the claims, Edward and I went up to Cherokee for the money for two interests. I had possession of one of my partner's interest for some money I had let him have. Turner, one of the new company, paid one thousand dollars, all in twenty dollar gold pieces. The rest was to be paid within a week. It was about five miles from Cherokee to our cabin, through the woods, and there were no houses or cabins on the road. When we started to return with the money, it was nearly dark. Turner wanted to know if we had a pistol. We said, "No." He advised us to take one of his, as he did not think it safe for us to go without one with so much money. Ed. took the pistol and went ahead a short distance. I followed with the money. I told Ed. if anyone said anything to him to shoot him on the spot, and I would run with the money. We arrived at the cabin in safety, not having seen anyone on the road.

Sherman wanted I should invest what spare money I had in real estate in Nevada City, saying that I could get better interest there than at home. I thought, however, I had better send it home, to replace the money I had brought with me. And lucky for me that I did, for Nevada City had a $2,000,000 fire shortly afterwards, which destroyed most of the city, and in which my brother Sherman lost his life.

One day, when Sherman was visiting us, he asked me if I would like to be superintendent of roads and streets in Grass Valley township. He said he could get the position for me, if I wanted it. I told him I could not attend to it, as I had all I could do to look after my various mining claims, for I had bought into a number of companies.

Our company on the Point claims bought a lot of lumber of Sam Robbins, now living in Carlisle in this state, for making two lines of sluice boxes about three hundred feet long, also a lot of plank and timber for "timbering up" an inclined shaft to prospect a quartz ledge we had found on our upper claims. Robbins hauled his logs to a saw mill, and took his pay in lumber, which he sold to miners, and anyone else wanting it. We could get the lumber much cheaper of him than at the saw-mill. It cost him nothing to keep his oxen; he would turn them out at night, and they would get plenty to eat, and would be ready to go to work in the morning. He put a bell on one of the oxen, so that he could find them in the morning. The land belonging to the government, and was free for everybody. There were plenty of trees for lumber all about the country.

Two of my partners had an interest in a quartz ledge on Church hill. I worked for this company part of the summer, during the dry season, when we had no water on our claims. They worked the claims day and night. The men that worked days one week, worked nights the next. Some of the owners worked in the mines with the help. It was cool in the drifts, a thing which made it pleasant working in summer.

One evening near the end of June 1856, as I was coming from the claims with a pail of water in my hand, I met two little girls who lived near our cabin, all out of breath from running. They said they were going to have a Fourth of July picnic. The children of Grass Valley, Nevada and Rough and Ready were going to assemble in a grove between Grass Valley and Nevada. The girls were to be dressed in white, the children were going to sing and have recitations. One of the Nevada lawyers was to read the Declaration of Independence, another was to deliver an oration. Lemonade was to be free, "and, Mr. Fletcher, won't you please give us some money?" I asked them how much they wanted, and they said two dollars. I gave them the money, and away they ran. After they had gone a few rods, however, they turned round and told me I must come to the celebration. Ed and I went to the picnic, and the programme was carried out about as the girls said. There was a good attendance, and everyone had a good time. The children sang some very pretty songs. One of the best singers was Dr. Thompson's daughter, of Grass Valley. It was not an uncommon thing for miners to go to the Methodist church for the purpose of hearing her solos in the choir. The boys spoke some very pretty pieces, and all drank lots of lemonade. In the afternoon Edward and I left the picnic and went to a horse-race at Huser's ranch, about two miles away. The race was between two rival stables in Nevada City. Lancaster, the owner of one of the stables, said he had the best horse in Nevada. This claim was disputed by another stable-keeper. The two horses were driven by two boys horseback. The first start was a false one, but the Lancaster horse went the whole length of the track before the boy could stop him. The next start was all right and the Lancaster horse won. We saw quite a number of miners of our acquaintance at the race.

On our return to Grass Valley we all went to an ice cream saloon, and treated one another to ice cream.

There were only about three hundred children in the procession at the picnic. Now there are fifteen hundred in Grass Valley alone, as I was informed when I was there in 1886.

## CHAPTER VI.

NEVADA FIRE. FURTHER EXPERIENCES IN MINING.

Soon after the Fourth of July, the water on one of our claims gave out, and four or five of our company, including myself, started on a prospecting tour in the mountains about six miles above Nevada, on Deer Creek, which runs through Nevada City. One of our partners had prospected there before with a pan, with very good results, as he thought; but the gold was scaly and difficult to hold in the sluice. We took a two-horse load of mining tools, provisions, blankets and mattresses with us. We found a deserted cabin near by, which we occupied while we were there. We worked the ground till the twentieth of July, but it did not pay to our satisfaction, and we made plans to return to Grass Valley. We did not work very hard; it was a kind of summer vacation for us.

The 19th of July, 1856, was Saturday. The next morning we were all late in getting up. A man living near by came from Nevada City, and as he passed by the cabin shouted out that Nevada City was nearly all burnt down, and quite a number had perished in the flames. S. W. Fletcher being, as he thought, one of the number, I started for Nevada as soon as possible without any breakfast. Arriving at a hill overlooking the city, I could see that it was nearly all destroyed. Some of the inhabitants were encamped on the hill where I was, having lost everything. The neighboring towns had to send them provisions to keep them from starving. Sacramento, San Francisco, and other cities sent them clothing, and money, also. Arriving at the ruins, I made inquiries for my brother, and soon found there was no doubt that he had perished in the flames. I procured a horse and started for Shady Creek to get Edward. I met him and Charlie Cornell coming into Nevada. We both went to Grass Valley for a few days, until the ruins should cool. The remains were found a day or two after the fire.

The funeral was from the house of Mr. Tweed, his partner. The lawyers of Nevada acted as pall-bearers, his friend Stewart being one of the number. It was Stewart who threw the first shovelful of dirt into my brother's grave, after the coffin had been lowered.

I had a talk with the man who last saw Sherman alive, and was in the building when the fire started, but saved himself by leaping out of a window. My brother's office was situated in a brick building, which was thought to be fire proof; the county records were kept here. On the first floor was a grocery store and a bank, kept by a man by the name of Hager, who perished in the flames. The second floor was taken up by offices and the room where the records were kept. The new court house was nearly finished, and at the time of the fire men were engaged in carrying the records there.

When the cry of fire was raised, the men in the building,

my brother among them, ran down into the street to see where it was. They found it was just behind the United States hotel, on the other side of the street, nearly opposite. They all ran back into the building to close the iron shutters. They then ran down to go out of the building. In the meanwhile someone had shut the iron door to prevent the fire from going into the building, not knowing there was any one inside. My brother found it impossible to open the iron door, since it had expanded with the heat. They then ran back to his office. The man who was saved told the rest he was going to leave the building. He jumped out of a rear window down upon a small building, and escaped without injury. He said Sherman was behind him, and supposed he would follow. Instead of doing that, he closed the window and iron shutters, supposing the building to be fire-proof. They all went into the basement, where they perished. All were burned beyond recognition, except Sherman. His remains were found, face down, in a passageway of a partition; the bosom of his shirt was not burned. He wore a gold specimen breastpin, which Edward gave him. This was the only thing to identify his remains. There was also a twenty dollar gold piece in his pocket. Two of his law books were saved. Tweed took one and I the other. The title of my book is "Angell on Water Courses."

From the *Boston Journal:*

"Nevada City in Ashes."—We copy the following telegraph despatch from *The California American:*

"Grass Valley, July 20, 1856, 1 A. M.—A fire broke out at four o'clock P. M. yesterday in the rear of Dr. Alban's fire-proof building on Pine Street, which spread to the adjoining building, occupied as a brewery. The wind favoring, it spread across to the United States Hotel and down and upward with great rapidity, taking the whole of Broad Street, Main Street, and all the cross streets, consuming all the express offices, banking houses, and churches, the new court house and County Recorder's office, stores, etc. The only buildings that have escaped are as follows: Dr. Alban's apothecary store, Dr. Lark's apothecary store, S. Miers' boot and shoe store, S. Hohlman's clothing store, and Potter's store.

"Persons burnt to death, as far as known: A. J. Hager, banker; J. Johnson, Ex-Deputy Surveyor; P. Hendrickson, merchant; S. W. Fletcher, late District Attorney; Wm. Anderson, of the Democrat; G. A. Young, merchant. Wm. Wilson, plasterer, burnt, but not fatally.

"The whole of the business part of the town is entirely consumed, commencing at the foot of Pine Street, extending up Spring to the junction of Broad Street, crossing below Womack's building to Washington bridge, thence across to High Street, down to Deer Creek, crossing to Little Deer Creek, below Lancaster's dwelling, and thence down Deer Creek to the foot of Pine Street, where it commenced—embracing from one hundred and fifty to two hundred acres of ground. The loss is variously estimated at from $2,000,000 to $3,000,000."

The following letter from Senator Stewart may be of interest.

UNITED STATES SENATE,
WASHINGTON, D. C., February 5, 1894.

D. C. FLETCHER, ESQ., Littleton, Mass.

*My Dear Sir:*—Your brother was a promising young lawyer and a most excellent man. If he had lived, he would certainly have taken a leading place at the bar, and been a most useful citizen. His untimely death in the great fire at Nevada City, California, in 1856, was a sad event. I was very intimate with him, and he often talked with me about his hopes and aspirations. I felt his death as a personal loss, and mourned him as a friend.

Yours very truly,

WM. M. STEWART.

Afterwards I went to San Francisco and procured a marble monument for brother's grave.

Edward and I visited Mr. Tweed's family Sundays for a long time. We were always kindly received and had a pleasant time.

On my way to San Francisco to procure my brother's monument, I fell in with a man of my acquaintance by the name of Ernest, and I persuaded him to go with me. We spent several days in seeing the sights. We visited the government fort on an island in the harbor. We hired a man to take us over in a rowboat, since no steamers went to the island in those days. It was a large fort with many guns mounted; it guarded the entrance to the Golden Gate.

We returned to Grass Valley together. It was the first time Ernest had seen the city, having crossed the plains in coming to California.

Late in the spring of 1857, after we had sold out our claims in Shady Creek, Edward and George Edmunds, one of our old partners, took the job of putting in a "cut," five hundred feet in length, on our old claims, receiving eighteen hundred dollars and what gold they could find. Sometimes it ran through a creek, where we found gold and quicksilver, but we did not know how much. At the lower end of the cut was a waterfall, made by a ledge, which would require considerable blasting. Ed. wrote to me at Grass Valley, asking me to go in with them. As the water on my claims would soon give out, I concluded to accept his offer, and went to work with them as soon as the water gave out. We had to have a derrick and blasting tools, such as drills, hammers, iron bars, powder and fuse, picks, shovels, etc. Most of these things we purchased in Grass Valley. The iron castings for the derrick we bought second hand at Shady Creek. We thought of procuring an anvil and sharpening our own tools, but finally made arrangements with a blacksmith near by to do this work. We took three kegs of powder with us from Grass Valley, but used nine kegs before we finished the cut. We hired a man of our acquaintance, a good fellow to work, to help us. We all lived in a log cabin, and boarded ourselves. I used to take the tools to the blacksmith to be sharpened before breakfast, so that the men could go to work by seven o'clock. I was anxious to have the work finished before the rainy season set in. When we were drilling holes for blasting, I held the drill. We had two to strike, and sometimes three. When the powder was put in, George held the tamping iron, while I used the hammer. We ought never to have used iron for tamping, but wood. None of us had ever had much experience in blasting. We got along very well with our work, till one morning when we were putting in a slanting blast. George was holding the tamping iron, as usual, and I was swinging the hammer. The blast went off before we had finished tamping, blowing the rock and powder into George's face and hands. Probably we cut the fuse. He stood up and told us to take him to the cabin. I saw he was badly hurt, and went for a doctor as fast as possible, while Ed. and the hired man helped him to the cabin.

I hurried to Oak Tree ranch, but finding nobody at home but the ladies, left word for the stage driver to send a doctor from San Juan, for it was nearly time for the Nevada stage. When the stage arrived, the driver ran his horses to San Juan as fast as they could go. I then started for Webb's ranch, a quarter of a mile up the road towards Cherokee, and told them to send to Cherokee for a doctor, also. I then returned to the cabin. When I came in sight of the cabin, I saw George walking about. Charlie Cornell was just coming over the creek to see how bad the accident was. We told George to stand still. As soon as he heard my voice, he inquired if I was hurt. I told him I was all right. Ed. and Robert, the hired man, after taking George up to the cabin, went back for me, expecting to find me badly hurt. Cornell said we had better take George over to his house, which we were very glad to do. Two doctors soon arrived. The one we picked out to take charge of George had been in the English navy. One finger was so badly injured that it had to be amputated. Both hands were badly injured, also, and the eyes most of all. The doctor thought he would have to lose one eye and perhaps both. He waited until the next morning before removing the little pieces of rock.

The doctor left word for the eyes to be washed out with a syringe every half hour. This was extremely painful. George begged of us not to do it so often, but we told him he ought to do as the doctor said. Ed. and I watched with him over night. He was out of his head part of the time. He would call to us, "Pull me out of that hole." When the doctor came the next morning, he found George much better than he expected. He said a piece of rock came so near the pupil of one eye that a hair's breadth would have destroyed it.

George stayed a few days at the Oak Tree ranch, then we moved him to San Juan, where the doctor lived, so that he could see him at any time. Edward stayed with him a month. The improvement was as rapid as could be expected. They both lived in a cabin by themselves, so as not to be disturbed by any one.

The company we were working for, when they heard of the accident, sent word to us that they would pay a man for taking care of George for a month, which they did, costing them one hundred and twenty-five dollars.

At the time of the accident a piece of rock hit me in the corner of one eye, and some rock and powder were blown into my chin, but the injuries were not serious enough to prevent me from working. Edward thought we had better give up the job. We had expended three or four hundred dollars on the cut up to the time George was hurt, and we would lose that if we did not finish the job. I said we must finish the cut, and we did.

We hired a man who understood the business of blasting, and paid him four dollars a day. Neither Ed, Robert nor I would put in a blast after the accident for love or money; we had got blasted out. We went over to see George every Sunday, and spent the day with him. He was in good spirits, and did not worry over his misfortunes, but he did not recover for over a year, and his eyes were weak after that.

We finished the cut that fall without any further accident, before the rainy season set in, to the satisfaction of the company. After we had finished the work, the company bought our derrick and all the tools we wanted to dispose of at a fair price, and paid us in a short time. They were good fellows, and we knew it when we took the contract.

With what gold and quicksilver we took out of the creek and the eighteen hundred dollars we were paid, we realized about two thousand five hundred dollars, making three dollars a day for our summer's work. We expected to make five dollars, but it was a more difficult job than we reckoned for. George's getting hurt put us back a good deal.

Soon after finishing the cut I returned to Grass Valley.

I was then taken sick in my cabin. Mr. Tweed, my brother's late law partner, hearing of my sickness, came to see me, and invited me to come to his house at Nevada City and stay until I recovered. I was very glad to accept the kind invitation, for a miner's cabin is a poor place to be sick in. He sent his carriage for me, and under the care of Mrs. Tweed, I soon recovered. The doctor wanted to know if I had not overworked. He told me I should be all right in a few weeks, which proved to be the case.

One time when I was at work on my point claims, before selling out at Shady Creek, Clark, one of my partners, came to me with a specimen which he had found while at work washing some tailings. It consisted of a quartz rock a little larger than my fist, one end of which was full of gold. The Day Company evidently had not seen the specimen when they worked the ground for the first time. I asked him how much it was worth, and he said between two hundred and fifty and three hundred dollars. We weighed it as well as we could, and estimated the value at two hundred and sixty-nine dollars. It was put up at auction, and knocked off to me for two hundred and seventy dollars. I intended to take it home with me, but having use for the money I crushed it, and realized two hundred and sixty-nine dollars, losing just about one dollar by the operation.

One Sunday morning I started for Shady Creek over the stage road, called Robinson's road, from the name of the man who had built it, and as I was drawing near the bridge over the South Yuba River, I met a suspicious looking man on horseback. He wore a big cape which covered him all up but his legs. After he had passed me, he suddenly stopped and asked me the time of day. I told him I did not know, still keeping my eyes on him and walking away as fast as I could. I thought the man intended to rob me. I had the specimen with me, which I was intending to show to Edward at Shady Creek. I didn't give him a chance, however, to get the "drop" on me. I arrived at Shady Creek, and my partners told me I had the best specimen they had seen for a long time. I came home by stage, as I did not care to encounter any more men in long capes, when I had the two hundred and seventy dollar specimen.

There was an old shaft on our upper claims full of water. Two years before all the miners in that vicinity used to clean up their gold here. It was supposed there were several hundred dollars in the shaft, as some gold is always wasted in cleaning up. One morning three men put a windlass in the shaft, and commenced cleaning it out. I told them the ground belonged to us, and forbade them working there. They said they used to "pan out" there, and so had the right to clean out the hole. I went down town to get the sheriff to stop them. One of the lawyers told me that it would cost ninety dollars to employ the sheriff, and it would take all day to execute the necessary papers. In the meanwhile the shaft would be cleaned out. He wanted to know where I was at work, and how many men I had. I told him on the Point claims, where ten or twelve men were working. He said they had no right to clean out the shaft, and advised me to take my gang and put the intruders off the ground. At noon we all went to where they were cleaning out the shaft, to see if we could not make them leave. I had a talk with them before we commenced operations. They finally consented to leave it out to three men. They were to appoint one man, I another, and the two a third. I told my man whom to have for the third man. He was a ditch agent and an old miner. The three men decided in my favor. I asked the men who were working on the shaft if they were satisfied, and they said they were, and left. Clark, my partner, was very indignant because I left it out. He said, "Put them off the ground." I told him it was better to leave it out, as no honest miner would decide against us, and besides all trouble would be avoided. We afterwards cleaned out the shaft, and realized between three and four hundred dollars.

## CHAPTER VII.

LAST DAYS IN CALIFORNIA.

Most of the people who went to California in 1849 and later, went to get a start in the world. Money was difficult to obtain in the East. Everybody wanted to get rich all at once. A great many steady and honest men became comfortably well off. Millionaires were scarce. Others who came there in '49 are there still, as poor as when they came.

My brothers and I did not travel about the country much except on business. I went to Dutch Flat twice, once in company with my partner Clark. We walked there, and a very rough road it was over the mountains. A railroad to the East was in contemplation about this time. I remember we all said a railroad could never be built where we went. The Central Pacific has a station at Dutch Flat; so we were mistaken that time.

In the spring of 1859 I had disposed of my mining interests, intending to return home during the year. A member of the Empire Company, Smith by name, told me about a quartz ledge he had discovered five miles from Omega, the last mining town this side of the Sierra Nevada mountains. He said he could see the gold in the quartz, and thought there was a good lead in the hill, and asked me to go up there and prospect, since he know I had had considerable experience in mining. I told him I expected to return East sometime during the year, but preferred to return late in the fall or in the winter, as that was the healthiest time to cross the Isthmus.

I made arrangements to run a tunnel into the hill, with the understanding that I could stop whenever I wanted to. In this way I could prospect the hill more thoroughly than by sinking a shaft. I had a man with me to wheel out the dirt. The tunnel was begun on the west side of the mountain overlooking the South Yuba River. We could see the river, more than two thousand feet below us We could see the waste rock that came out of the tunnel roll down the mountain a long distance.

We had been working about a week, when we had a call from some men, who said we were destroying their flume with the rock that came out of the tunnel. We told them we did not know that any flume was there, and could not see it from the mouth of the tunnel. They said we had destroyed five or six of their boxes. We told them we would pay for what damage we had done. They said they would not ask us to do that, if we would not destroy any more of the flume, which we agreed to. We managed to pile up the rocks at the mouth of the tunnel, so that they did not run down the mountain.

This flume was part of a ditch that was being built to convey water from the head waters of the South Yuba to Grass Valley and Nevada City. One company had failed, having spent $20,000 in the undertaking. Another company then took hold of it, and put it through. There is now plenty of water in Nevada and Grass Valley all the year round for all kinds of purposes. The quartz mills use it to run their machinery, since it is much cheaper than steam power. The residents use it in their houses, paying about two dollars a month for it.

The company constructing the ditch had a mill near where we were at work, to saw lumber for the flume. They used 1,000,000 feet for building a flume to carry the water over the difficult places in the mountains, where they could not build a ditch.

On the Fourth of July I followed the ditch to the head waters of the South Yuba. I could see snow on the mountains. The ditch was about six feet wide and three or four feet deep. These ditches are given a fall of only a quarter of an inch to the rod, so as not to wash out the banks.

We lived in a deserted cabin not far from our work. The man that worked with me came from Columbus, Mississippi. He had been engaged in the grocery business before he came to California. We had many arguments about slavery. He was pro-slavery to the backbone. We were disputing one night in an animated manner after we had retired; he said he would get up and go out back of the cabin and fight it out, if I was willing,—and he meant it. I told him we didn't settle disputes in that way in the North. He was a large, powerful man, and could whip two men of my size at the same time. He said the laboring people of the North were no better than slaves. We could never agree when we talked about slavery. We used to go to Omega every week to get the news and mail, and to order things for the cabin. One day some trappers brought in a grizzly bear they had caught in a trap. They had him in an iron cage. They sold him at Marysville for fifty dollars for a bull and bear fight.

We worked several months in the tunnel without finding any quartz ledge. The ground had become so hard that we could not work any more without blasting, and I was unwilling to blast in a tunnel after my experience in blasting in the open air, and, besides, I was getting impatient to start for home. One day I bought of a man who came to the cabin, a watermelon two feet long. It was one of the sweetest melons I ever ate. Late in the fall I went to Grass Valley and informed the owners of the mine that I wanted to quit work and return East. He settled with me, and I started at once for San Francisco. Before I left, Edward and I went to Dutch Flat to visit Mr. Tweed's family. The Tweeds expected to return East soon to see a brother, who was a professor in Tufts College. My brother decided to stay in California.

I stopped at the What Cheer House in San Francisco. As I came out of the dining-room one evening, I met an old schoolmate from Massachusetts, named Fletcher. We went to the fire engine house parlor and had a long talk about Littleton and its people. He sold papers in California, and found it a paying business. The engine house had a parlor, sitting-room and library for the use of its men. A brother of this Fletcher recently left the Littleton Library one thousand dollars.

My ticket took me home through Panama. On the way to Panama I met a man who was on the steamship Independence when it was burned, and many lives lost, on the way from San Francisco to Panama. When the captain found he could not save the ship he went as near shore as possible; the passengers jumped from the boat on the land side, but those who could not swim clung to those who could, causing the death of many. My friend jumped off on the ocean side, and swam around the others, and so escaped.

When about a day's sail from Panama we were enveloped in a heavy thick fog, which prevented us from seeing the length of the ship. We were near an island, but as it could not be exactly located, we went very slowly, sometimes stopping. Many officers and sailors were stationed on different parts of the ship on the lookout, one forward, and one on each side of the ship. The fog lifted a little. I happened to be looking straight ahead at the time, and saw the island directly in front of us. There was a great commotion on board for a few minutes. The ship was turned to the left as soon as possible to clear the island. If the fog had not lifted as it did we should probably have been wrecked. Everett Hoar, one of our neighbors at home, was wrecked on that island, or another island in that vicinity, a few years later, on a voyage to California. I think the passengers were all saved, but they were obliged to stay on the island several months, living on stores obtained from the wreck. They were picked up by another ship sent out to find them. We arrived at Panama without any other mishap. I went to see the Spaniard who kept the hotel where my brother Theodore and I stopped on our way to California. He was still keeping the hotel, but did not look well. We stopped at Acapulco, Mexico, on our way down, where I purchased a lot of sea shells. I also purchased two very nice ones at Panama. Most of them I have given away to my friends.

We arrived at Panama about ten o'clock in the morning, and went on shore in boats. There was no improvement in leaving and going on board ships, on account of a ledge of rocks in the harbor. We crossed the Isthmus in two or three hours by the Panama railroad. The trains stop at Aspinwall on the same wharf where the steamship leaves for New York.

The gold dust that came on our ship, amounting to $1,000,000 or $2,000,000, the baggage and freight, were all transported across the Isthmus and loaded on the New York boat in one day. We arrived at Panama in the morning, and I could just see land on the other side the next morning, as we sailed for New York. The only thing to do after arriving in New York was to go home. It was a sad returning this time. Death had entered our family circle for the first time. For during my absence my brother Sherman had lost his life in the Nevada fire, and George, another brother, had died at home in 1857. I at once wrote to Edward in California, informing him of my safe arrival home.

At the time of the War of the Rebellion my brother Edward enlisted in a company that recruited in Nevada

City. They joined a California regiment, expecting to be sent to the front. The Indians, however, were so troublesome in Southern California that they were detained there. When his three years of service had expired, he was stationed in a fort in Arizona. By permission of the commander of the fort, Edward and a man by the name of Brown opened a store near the fort. After leaving the service they ran an express and pack train from Mohave City in Arizona to Los Angeles in Southern California, about three hundred miles through the wilderness. Their train consisted of forty mules and horses. On one occasion the Indians stampeded the train at some point on the route, and ran the animals all off but five. Ed. and Brown and the men who helped run the pack, sixteen in number, put after the Indians, and followed them for three days and three nights into the mountains. A big rain and hail storm came on, and being out of provisions, they had to abandon the pursuit. They recovered most of the animals, but they were dead; for the Indians killed them, if they could not keep them from being recaptured. Edward on this occasion caught a very bad cold, which settled on his lungs, and he never recovered. He stayed at Los Angeles a year, but did not grow any better. He then went to San Francisco, intending to go to the Sandwich Islands. But he was so feeble that he thought he had better come home, if he ever expected to see father and mother again. He arrived home about the first of December, 1868, and died on Christmas day, living but three weeks after arriving in Massachusetts.

# PART SECOND.

## THE WAR OF THE REBELLION.

### CHAPTER VIII.

#### ENLISTMENT, 1861.

And now came the Rebellion of 1861-65, in which the young men of the country were obliged to take a conspicuous part. Of course the Fletcher family of Littleton, who were bound to have a hand in every good work, were not behindhand this time. I have spoken of my brother Edward's enlistment in the preceding pages. I was the only young man at home unmarried, and it appeared to be my duty to go to the war. I was in excellent health after my return from California, and felt myself able to stand any number of hard knocks. Besides the above reasons for enlisting I was influenced to a considerable extent by the state of public opinion. The pulpit and the press were ablaze with patriotism. The selectmen, and in fact all the prominent men of the town, urged the young men to enlist. One of the selectmen told me he thought I ought to go to the war first, and he would come after me. Another prominent man in town said that blood would be shed, as both sides, North and South, had "got their dander up," but thought I ought to go and defend the right.

The way I came to enlist was in connection with selling some apples in Boston. When I was in California, mining, one of my partners told me that winter apples packed in plaster would keep in good condition until June. Accordingly in the fall of 1860 I packed eight or ten barrels of apples in plaster, and put them in the cellar. Late in April, 1861, when the whole country was arming on account of the fall of Fort Sumter, I opened the barrels, and found the apples had decayed more than those that had not been packed in plaster. I made the best of it, however, and after cleaning off the plaster and packing them over, started with the best of them for Boston with father's team, intending to find some regiment to enlist for the war. After arriving in Boston, I found a number of three-years' regiments recruiting for the war, among them the 11th and 12th Massachusetts. I happened to go into the hall where the 11th was recruiting, near Bowdoin Square. I put my name down as intending to be one of their number. I was not enlisted into the regiment, however. I was told I had better not leave the city if I intended to go with them, as they expected to leave for Washington in a few days. I left the team in a stable, and wrote to father to send for it.

The regiment drilled in the hall, for a week, in the step and facings, and then were ordered down to Fort Warren to drill. The companies were not full. I did not like the idea of going down to Fort Warren, as I wanted to go to the front at once. Nor did I like the way the officers were chosen. So I began to look around to find some other organization. I was standing in the doorway of the drill-hall one day, when a man asked me if I would not like to go to West Cambridge, (now Arlington,) and join a company that was forming there. He gave me such a flattering account of the company that I concluded to go and see about it. I was also advised to go to West Cambridge by my brother Theodore, who had come down to Boston with some hay, and had dropped in at the hall of the 11th Regiment to see me. So we all three rode to West Cambridge in Theodore's hay wagon. I was told that the company would assemble in the evening in the town hall. I was on hand, and was so well pleased with everything, that I joined the company. I stayed with them till wounded in 1862. Captain Albert S. Ingalls, who was getting up the company, with the help of the town, was a prominent lawyer of West Cambridge.

The members of the company who did not live in town, boarded at the hotel, the town paying the bills. Later I boarded with a man by the name of Hill. His only son was a member of the company, and was killed in '62. I was not acquainted with any of the company, but found it on the whole rather pleasant to meet so many strangers and form new acquaintances. Most of the company lived in town, or in the neighboring towns. A number of Addison Gage's ice-men joined the company. Albert S. Ingalls was elected captain, Frank Gould, first lieutenant, John Locke and Charlie Graves were commissioned officers, either in our company, or in some other company of the regiment which we joined later. The town furnished us with uniforms and other things that we needed. We drilled in the town hall afternoon and evening, and sometimes in a vacant lot in the daytime. One day the company marched to Belmont and took the cars for Boston, to procure muskets. We marched all the way back by way of Charlestown and Winter Hill. We attended church in a body on Sundays at the Unitarian church, then at the Orthodox and Baptist, on invitation.

There being no vacancy for a company in any regiment then forming in the state, we had permission from the governor to join a regiment in Brooklyn, New York. We started the last of May for New York. The company assembled in the town hall, and were provided with knapsacks and blankets, and also given seven dollars each in money. The ladies of the town furnished us with towel, soap, pins, needles and thread, and other little things not provided by the government. The last thing we received was a testament, given us by the Orthodox minister. We went by way of Fall River and Long Island Sound. Two companies joined us at Fall River, one from Milford, Captain Lindsay, the other from Newburyport, Captain Wescott. The three companies were to join the same regiment at Brooklyn. Arriving in New York the three companies marched to the Astor House and took breakfast. We were quartered in three halls in Brooklyn, one for each company, taking our meals at a hotel near by. Everything was first class. The regiment we were to join was not ready, and from all appearances would not be for several weeks. The captains of the companies wrote to the governor of Massachusetts for instructions, and we were ordered home again, after staying in Brooklyn somewhat less than a week.

Upon our arrival in Boston, Captain Ingalls received orders from the selectmen of West Cambridge to come back to the town and stay there at the town's expense until we found another chance to go to the front. The captain said he would not take the company back to West Cambridge until they had seen some fighting. The company went down to Fort Warren, and stayed one night. We then boarded at a hotel in Boston a number of days. In the meanwhile the three captains had heard of another regiment in Yonkers, New York, that was not full. They at once went to Yonkers to see what the prospect was. When they returned, they gave a favorable report, and we all started at once for Yonkers. Upon our arrival we found the Mozart Regiment, 40th New York, recruiting for the war. It was a New York City regiment, gotten up by Mayor Fernando Wood. The three Massachusetts companies joined the regiment. Later Captain Wescott raised another company in Lawrence, Mass., which joined this regiment. We were stationed in a large brick building at Yonkers, recruiting, none of the companies having the full quota of officers and men. We used to go up the Hudson River on the steamers, visiting the towns situated along the river. Some of us went to Sing Sing, where the state prison is located. The superintendent invited us in to see the prisoners take dinner. There were one thousand of them in the dining-hall. Officers were stationed in different parts of the room to take care of them. If one prisoner had too much bread or meat, the officer was signaled by signs, and it was given to another prisoner who did not have enough. We tasted some of the bread and found it very good. We were shown about the prison by the officers· It cost us nothing to go where we pleased on the boats, except to New York City. With a number of others I visited the spot where Major Andre was captured during the Revolution. The spot was in the woods near a brook, and was marked by a monument to commemorate the event. We usually went in squads of five or six, taking a lieutenant with us, if we could, and were usually invited to dinner by some of the citizens of the places we visited. One day five of us went up to Peekskill to see the place. About one o'clock we were talking with one of the citizens, when he asked us if we had had any dinner. We told him, "No." He then invited us to dine at his house. We accepted the invitation with thanks. As we entered the dining-room, a young lady left the room. After dinner, as we left the front yard through the gate, the young lady was there, and gave each of us a rose. She said she had a brother in the army.

Tents were furnished us, and we went into camp a week before we left for Washington. Before we went into camp, the ladies of Yonkers treated us to strawberries and cream. I heard that the ladies furnished the strawberries, and the merchants of Yonkers the sugar and cream. We had all we wanted,—at least, I did. I had eaten one plateful, and went into line for another. One of the ladies, who passed the strawberries to the soldiers, asked me if I had not been there before. I gave an evasive reply. She said she thought there would be enough, and gave me another plate. I heard that two or three bushels were left over after the soldiers had eaten all they wanted.

In the afternoon of June 27, we were sworn into the United States' service for three years or during the war. Each company had to number one hundred and one officers and men, before it could be mustered in. The next morning the orderly sergeant informed me that I had been appointed by the captain one of the corporals,—an agreeable surprise to me. The five sergeants and eight corporals of each company are appointed by the captain. There were ten companies in each regiment. The sergeants and corporals act as police in each company. In line of battle the captain, first and second lieutenants, and four sergeants are two paces in rear of the company, to keep the men in their places. The orderly sergeant takes the captain's place at the head of the company. The lieutenant-colonel, major and adjutant are a few paces in the rear of the company officers and sergeants. The colonel is in the rear of the regiment. The first duty I had to perform, after being appointed corporal, was to put a man in the guard-house. He was talking, and made considerable unnecessary noise. I told him to "shut up," and exercised considerable authority, more than I afterwards did when arresting a man. Quite a number were looking on to see me operate, and I thought I must show as much authority as possible to make them believe I was somebody.

Once at midnight while we were in camp at Yonkers, the long roll was beat. The regiment was in line as soon as possible. Mayor Wood had come up to our camp from New York City. He wanted to see how quickly the regiment could be assembled. We were all in bed at the time, except the guard. He made a speech to the regiment, and complimented us upon getting into line so promptly at midnight. The first night we were in camp at Yonkers I woke up and could see the stars. Some one had pulled up the tent pins, and let the tent down on us. There was in our tent a man who was always finding fault with everybody,—cross, and nothing ever went right with him. Otherwise he was a good fellow enough. We thought the tent was pulled down for his special benefit. Of course he made a great fuss, and wanted to know who pulled up the tent pins, etc. I told him to help put up the tent, and not to make such a noise about it. I tented with somebody else after that. He died at Camp Sacket in the winter of '61–'62. His body was embalmed, and sent home to his friends, together with his personal property. The company paid all expenses, which amounted to about one hundred dollars. The privates and non-commissioned officers paid half a dollar each, the lieutenants ten dollars, and the captain twenty dollars. The captain said no more bodies would be sent home, since it was too great a tax on the company. He was the first man in the company to die. He lived in Gorham, Maine, and left a wife and three children.

On the Fourth of July we started for Washington. All the ten companies that composed the regiment were mustered into the United States' service. We were supplied with everything we wanted, and more than we could use. Many things were thrown away when we came to march. All the soldier wants when in active service, besides his equipments, is one hat, one woolen blanket, one rubber blanket, two woolen shirts, two pairs of socks, haversack, canteen, and one of those little bags of things that the ladies of Arlington gave us, and a testament.

Our camp at Yonkers was situated about a mile back of the town. The regiment marched down through the town with a band of music. Every one cheered us, and the ladies waved their handkerchiefs. The inhabitants of Yonkers had been very kind to us while we had been with them. The regiment took a steamboat for Jersey City, where we took the cars for Washington. We did not all get on board the boat at Yonkers till late in the afternoon. When we came in sight of New York, it was night. We could see the fireworks in the city as we passed by, in honor of the day. We made a stop in Philadelphia of an hour or more. When we left Yonkers, we had rations of hard bread and salt beef. I did not like this fare very well, and when we arrived at Philadelphia, I started out to see if I could not get something better. I asked at a number of houses in the suburbs for some milk, but they had none. At last I found a woman who had plenty. She told me to come in, and she gave me all the pie and cake I could eat, and all the milk I could drink. She also gave me pies, cake and a canteen full of milk to take to the cars for the other soldiers. I asked her what her bill was, and she said "Nothing." I told her I expected to pay for what I had. Still she refused any money. She said she had a son in the army. Good woman! I hope her son returned to her safe and sound.

I went to the cars pretty well loaded down with good things for the soldiers. The engine whistle blew fifteen or twenty minutes before we started for Washington. We had to go round through York, Pennsylvania, a roundabout way to get to Washington, the direct route not yet being established for government troops. We saw pickets out for the first time, beside the railroad from York to Washington. We went through Baltimore in the night. The streets were quiet, and our muskets were not loaded. On our arrival at Washington we went into camp about three miles this side of the city, and commenced drilling again, twice a day. Other regiments were encamped near us, also cavalry and artillery; all were getting ready for war. Sometimes when the soldiers were not on duty, they would pick blackberries in the neighboring fields. We used to give the cook some of them, and receive sugar in return to eat with the remainder. I went into the city a number of times to see the place. It was a great sight for one who had never been there before. The dome of the capital was not finished at this time, but men were working on it. It was finished before the close of the war.

Discipline was very lax at this time. I could get leave to go to Washington most any time. On the 21st of July, which was Sunday, we were encamped the other side of the Potomac, between Fort Ellsworth and the river. The chaplain of the regiment was holding services under a tree by the river. I was present. I whispered to Corporal Shepard, who sat next to me, that I thought there was a fight going on somewhere. We could hear the booming of cannon in the distance. The first battle of Bull Run had begun.

In the afternoon our regiment was ordered out and marched down to the railroad station at Alexandria. We took the cars to the west in the direction of Bull Run. The regiment guarded the railroad this side of Bull Run all night. Our orders were to shoot the first man who molested the railroad or telegraph. Late in the afternoon a train of cars came back from the direction of Bull Run. Some of the soldiers asked the conductor what the news was from the front. He said our troops were victorious. At daylight we saw troops coming down the railroad from the direction of Bull Run battlefield. They said our boys had been defeated, and the army had been ordered back to Washington. They were not running, neither did I see any other troops running on that day. They told us we had better hurry back to Washington, for the rebel Black Horse Cavalry were coming. We heard a good deal at this time about the Black Horse Cavalry, but saw nothing of them. About noon we took the cars back to Alexandria and returned to camp.

Soon after the Bull Run defeat our regiment was marched to Alexandria to guard the city. The regimental headquarters were in the court house. Thousands of troops were in the city. Regiments and companies were all mixed up. Everybody appeared to go wherever he pleased. But it did not take long for the soldiers to find their regiments. Notices were posted about the streets, stating where the headquarters of the different regiments were. I was corporal of the guard part of the time the regiment was guarding the city. One day, in the forenoon, there was a call for the corporal of the guard from post seventeen, down at the lower end of the city. The officer of the guard told me to take my musket and go down to post seventeen and see what was wanted. It was quite a walk down to the post. On my way down I met the President, Secretary Seward and General McDowell in a carriage coming up the street from Washington, going toward the Marshall House, where Ellsworth had been killed some weeks before. They saluted me when I met them. I appreciated the compliment. When I came to post seventeen, I found the soldier in charge had stopped a citizen. Some soldiers had been stealing hens from the citizen's hen-coop. The hens went up past the post, the soldiers in full pursuit of them. The owner of the hens was after the soldiers, but the hens and the soldiers were going so fast, they could not be stopped, but as the owner's rate of speed wasn't as great, he could be stopped; consequently the soldiers got the hens. I inquired what the orders were, and was told to stop everybody who hadn't the password. I told him to do as he was ordered. The citizen wished me to take dinner with him, but he looked so ugly I feared he would poison me, so I declined. When I reported the affair at headquarters, the men laughed, and thought it a neat way of getting the hens.

At midnight a soldier came running into headquarters saying, "For God's sake give me some hard tack." He claimed he had been in the battle of Bull Run, and had been in the woods without food ever since. We gave him all the beef, hard bread and coffee he wanted, and found him a place to sleep. He was very scared, and wanted to know if we thought the rebels would attack us before morning. We told him he would be awakened in season to run again, if the rebels came. He was the only scared man I saw from the Bull Run fight. We saw the same man at Second Bull Run, he having run away from his regiment again. The cavalry, that was on duty for just such soldiers, stopped him and sent him to his regiment. He had tried to join our regiment when we enlisted, but the captain, not liking his appearance, refused him. He was awkward, and did not learn the manual readily. Too much time was taken getting anything into his head.

## CHAPTER IX.

### CAMP LIFE AROUND WASHINGTON IN 1861.

After the Bull Run fight the rebels were very bold. At one time a rebel ran along the street, and fired into our camp in broad day light. Our men tried to catch him, but failed. The long roll, the signal of alarm, was beaten in our camp every night. We had to sleep with our clothes and equipments on, and a loaded musket by our side every night for some time. One night we were called in company line three times. The captain had two men stationed on the company street every night to get the men up as quick as possible when the long roll was beat.

The rebels were on Munson's hill in sight of Washington. Our soldiers built some forts and from these we soon drove the rebels back. Barracks were built inside the forts under ground, covered with logs and dirt to the depth of four feet. Here the soldiers slept, and here the wounded would be carried.

A soldier was hung at Fort Ellsworth, near Alexandria, for killing a negro woman, while he was drunk. He left a family at home. Many regiments were marched near the fort to witness the execution, ours being among them. No more negro women were killed by the soldiers after that.

Soon after Bull Run our company went on picket duty for the first time. I had charge of a picket post consisting of five men. My orders were to stop everyone not having a pass signed by a certain general. My post was stationed on the road. One man marched up and down for ten rods, night and day. He was relieved every two hours. The other men were allowed to smoke or sleep, but could not go away to their own tent. If one of the men went out of sight of the others, he took his musket. The first morning I was on picket duty, I saw an ambulance bringing in a man who had been killed by one of the guards. This man went outside the picket line. While he was gone, the picket was changed, and the new man on the post was not informed that a man was out. As the poor fellow came near the guard, he was told to halt three times, but as no response was made the guard fired, killing the man instantly.

When anybody comes near the guard, no matter if it be the corporal of the guard, he is told to "Halt and give the countersign." If the person doesn't stop, the guard retreats. Upon the continued approach of the man, the guard repeats "Halt" three times, retreating each time, and then fires.

One time a negro came up the road with a pass signed by the wrong general. I told him he could go no further with that pass. He said he had always been where he wanted to with the pass. I told two of my men to take their muskets and take the man to headquarters, where the captain was. I saw no more of the negro after that.

Late in the afternoon the officer of the picket came to the post, and told me I had better move my men to some other locality after dark; he said the rebels might find out where we were in the daytime, and attack us in the night, if we stayed there. I moved the men back to another place after dark. The corporal or sergeant who had charge of the post relieved the guard; so it was difficult for the one who had charge of the post to get much sleep. The first night I did not sleep at all, but the second night, managed to get a little sleep. At first I found it hard to keep the sentinels from going to sleep at their posts; but after threatening to send them to headquarters if they fell asleep again, I had no further trouble. At another time I had charge of the outside picket post, which was very disagreeable, as well as dangerous. The man who had charge of the post, has the pass-word ; the picket does not. If anyone came along, I had to go and see if he had the pass-word. Any little noise would startle me, so that I got very little sleep. But such times do not come to the same person very often.

At another time our reserve picket was near a house, where a man lived with his wife and sister. They were disloyal. One day the two women went to Alexandria to do some shopping. On their way back they were stopped and searched. Papers were found on them, from rebels in Washington, giving information to the enemy. They were both put in jail in Washington. A guard was put around the house day and night. The second night we were there, it was wet and cold. Accordingly, the captain, who was not feeling well, asked permission of the man who stayed in the house after the arrest of the women, to pass the night there. The man refused. Soon after the man sent word that he wanted some wood. The captain told him he might burn up his secession principles to keep warm. Before night he sent word to the captain that he might sleep in the house if he would furnish some wood. The captain sent a guard with the wood to see that the man did not communicate with the rebels. The captain then had a good night's sleep in the house. We were on picket two days and three nights at that time.

During the winter our regiment went on picket once in three weeks. At another time I was on the reserve picket, which is a more pleasant duty than having charge of a picket post, since the reserve pickets have plenty of time to sleep. We were stationed in an old plantation house. The overseer's house and quite a number of the negroes' houses were near by. There was nobody about the building but the overseer's wife and two or three small children. The woman said her husband was in Richmond jail on account of being a Union man. The colonel put a guard round the house so as to have her property saved. The woman was given things she needed to support her family. There were large quantities of corn on the place in bins, which our teams carried away.

We soldiers went up in the garret and found a large number of old deeds and mortgages, some of them dating back to the seventh century. Some of the soldiers sent these old papers home as relics of the place. At night some of us put some straw we found in the barn in the rooms up stairs, built a fire in the fireplaces, and had a warm, pleasant place to sleep. The officers occupied the rooms below. Some of the soldiers up stairs, without the knowledge of the officers, and in the night when everything was quiet, would roll stones down the stairs, waking up everybody in the house. After awhile an officer came to the foot of the stairs and told us not to roll any more stones. When everything was quiet, again they let another go. Bump, bump, bump, it went down to the bottom of the stairs, making a great racket. The officer then came up stairs and asked some men who were warming themselves by the fire, if they knew who rolled the stone down the stairs. Of course they said they did not. The officer said he would put us all in the guard-house if they rolled any more. The soldiers thought it best to keep quiet after that.

At three o'clock the next morning our company went outside the picket line on a scouting tour. The captain deployed a few men as skirmishers, so as not to be surprised by the enemy. We did not see anyone all the time we were gone, however. We went near enough to the rebels to hear their drums. There was ice in a brook that we crossed. We passed by the church where George Washington used to go to meeting. At another time we went on picket duty near a house where a man lived with his wife and three or four children. They were very poor and ignorant. I asked one of the boys what his father's name was. He said, "John." I asked what the rest of it was. He said that was all the name he had. The rebels tried to make John join their army, but he would not. There was no reading of any kind in the house, neither book nor newspaper, but the man knew enough to be a Union man.

In the fall of 1861, I had a visit from my brother Theodore. I got leave to go about with him the afternoon of the day he arrived. We went as far as the outside picket, where we were stopped by the sentinel. At night one of my tent-mates found another place to sleep, so that my brother could stay with me. When I asked if he slept well, he said, "No, somebody was tramping around all night." The guard was relieved every two hours, and this was the noise he heard. The next morning I got a pass from the captain to be gone all day, but he told me it must be signed by the colonel and Brigadier-general Sedgwick. The colonel refused to sign it for later than two o'clock, as at that hour we had a battalion drill and every man had to be on hand. Finally the captain prevailed on the colonel to sign it, and I was free until five o'clock. My brother and I saw the caval-cavalry and artillery drill. Theodore went into Fort Ellsworth, but my pass did not permit me to do so. We also went to Munson's Hill, where the rebels were after the Bull Run fight, and down to Long Bridge. I found the time limit of my pass was over, and I was five miles from camp. We had some oysters, and after bidding my brother a hasty good bye, I left on the double-quick. The next time I saw him, I was minus one leg. I got a little ride from a milkman, but did not go to the main entrance of the camp, fearing I should be detained. I managed to get through the guard by means of some brush and reached my tent safely. I had been in my tent but a short time when the orderly sergeant came to look for me. Lucky for me I was there. Orders were very strict at this time, and any known disobedience of headquarter orders, by officers or men, was severely punished.

Our corps, the third, was reviewed by the corps commander, General Heintzelman, two or three times during the fall. These reviews were very tedious to the soldiers, but were of benefit to the army in many ways, and not least because they gave us an opportunity to become acquainted with one another.

Late in the fall a review of the whole army was held by the President, General McClellan, the commander-in-chief, and other dignitaries. The army at this time numbered about 100,000 men. The pickets were doubled, as the rebels would probably hear of the review and might attempt a surprise. Our colonel made everyone go that could possibly leave, cooks, teamsters and some of the sick. He liked to have the regiment as large as possible at these reviews, so as to make a fine appearance. I was not very well at the time of the big review, but wanted to go very much, as it would be a big sight. I managed to get through the review, and then left the ranks, returning to camp at my leisure. The review was very imposing. The regiments marched two companies front, close order by divisions. Every one had a high opinion of the commanding officer, "Little Mac." I never saw the troops much better. When we marched by the reviewing officers, the divisions were as straight as a line. Everybody did his best.

The 40th Regiment, N. Y. V., gave the commanding officer three hearty cheers, as he passed in review. General McClellan reined up his horse, and raised his hat. I believe the Mozart Regiment could cheer louder than any other regiment in the service. Addison Gage, the proprietor of the ice company at Arlington, came out to see the company in the fall of 1861. He had a nephew in the company.

While we were at Camp Sacket, Governor Andrew sent a man with a paper for the officers and men of our company to sign, to see if they would not like to be transferred to a Massachusetts regiment. Lieutenant Gould and some of the non-commissioned officers, and many privates signed the paper; but I did not. They were tried by court-martial for insurrection, and found guilty. The lieutenant was dismissed from the service. The non-commissioned officers were reduced to the ranks. The colonel afterwards remitted the sentence, and all were restored to their old places in the company.

At one time the colonel was put under arrest for a week for forcing the guard. He had been visiting the 4th Maine, and on his return, refused to halt, and give the countersign at the command of the guard. The case was reported to General Sedgwick, who ordered his arrest. The colonel was not allowed to wear his sword or have any communication with his regiment, or to leave his tent. At the end of the week he was colonel of the regiment again. At another time the captain of our company was put under arrest for a week, for leaving his men, who were on fatigue duty, to a lieutenant, and going out with a large scouting party, consisting of three regiments of infantry, some cavalry and a battery. The captain, too, could not leave his tent, wear his sword or have any communication with his company for a week. After the week had expired, he was restored to his rank. I went out with the same scouting party. I was corporal of the guard at the time, and got another corporal to take my place, as I wanted to go with the boys very much. I suppose I should have been put under arrest, or put in the guard-house, if I had been found out. It was hard work for volunteers, both officers and men, to do just what they were ordered.

General Sedgwick, a West Point man commanded our brigade, and we had to obey orders, or there was trouble. The scouting party went near enough to the enemy to hear their drums. At the end of our march some of the soldiers knocked at the door of a house near by. There was no answer; the door was locked. The soldiers looking back a few minutes later, saw that the door was partly opened and someone was looking through the crack. They went back and inquired if they had any hens or ducks for sale. Two women came out of the house, when they found we were not going to rob them, and let some ducks out of the barn, and sold them to us for a dollar apiece. Soon after a man come out of the house, and asked us for tobacco. We gave them some, and then he and the women filled some pipes out of their pockets and went to smoking. They were the hardest looking women I ever saw,—tall, lank and cadaverous looking. They then wanted to buy some sugar and coffee, but we had none to sell or give away. They said they had been trying to get some for three weeks, but without success. We returned to camp about two o'clock in the morning. Our scouting cavalry had been fired at a number of times, and some of them wounded, and the scouting party had been ordered out to see if the rebels had put up any forts or earth-works near by. We found none, neither did we see any rebel soldiers.

About the first of November we went into winter quarters. The captain and lieutenants had tents facing and opposite the company streets. The sergeants and corporals tented at the head of the company streets, usually four in a tent. Corporals Shepard, Hammond and Braslin tented with me. For our house in winter we dug a hole in the ground two feet deep, and large enough for a tent to cover. We then built up two feet of logs on the edge, and covered it with our tent. We were provided with a new tent. Application was made at headquarters for our old tent, also, which was granted. We made an oven in one corner, of mud, rocks and sand on the side, with a big, flat rock on top. For a door we had a small flat rock. We made a chimney of sticks and mud outside the tent, communicating with the oven inside. Virginia mud makes very good brick after it is baked, so that we had a very good habitation, considering it was war times. There were two bunks in the tents, one above the other. For bedding we had a mattress and woolen blankets. Shepard and I occupied the upper bunk, Hammond and Braslin the lower one. When we were cold we built up a big fire, so that we did not suffer from the cold. Each man had a tin dipper, a tin plate, knife and fork, and a spoon to eat with. Each company had a cook-tent and a cook, who cooked for the whole company except the captain and lieutenants, who lived by themselves. The captain had a cook of his own, who procured his provisions of the brigade commissary.

We had in our company a man who had once been a cook in a restaurant in Boston, and the captain detailed him cook every week, at the request of the company. Nearly every soldier gave twenty-five cents to the cook every two months, so that he made double wages. This was given voluntarily. A few did not give anything to the cook, but they did not get any of the nice plum pudding and other delicacies which the cook used to prepare from time to time. Hiring the cook proved a good investment for the company, for owing to his skilful management we soon had a hundred dollar company fund from rations we did not draw from the government, besides having our food well cooked. We had baked beans quite often. The cook used to exchange some of our salt beef with some other company for beans. I think I never ate better beans than we had at Camp Sacket in the winter of 1861–62. The cook used to put in a hole dug in the ground a copper kettle large enough to hold a bushel or more. A fire was made in the hole, so that it was very hot. He put fifteen pounds of pork on top of the beans in the kettle, put the kettle in the hole and packed around it a lot of small, hot rocks. The beans were then covered up with an iron cover, and a fire was built on top. This was done at sundown. There was a guard at the cook-tent, day and night, and he was requested to keep a fire on top of the beans all night. The next morning Company H had baked beans good enough for a king. The colonel was up late one night, as he frequently was, to see what was going on in the regiment, and saw the fire at our cook-tent. He inquired of the guard, "What is that fire down at Company H's cook-tent?" The guard said they were cooking beans. "Company H is always cooking beans," he replied. He then went to bed. We sent him over a plateful the next morning. We had a loaf of good bread every day. It was said to be baked in the basement of the capital for the whole army. One of our four-horse wagons went down for our share every afternoon. The loaf of bread was usually more than I could eat in one day. We had fresh beef every week, and I think potatoes. Still we did not live so well as at home, and the soldiers used to buy pie, cake and other things of the sutler. The company was called together for their meals by the orderly sergeant. They were marched down to the cook-tent, in charge of the sergeant or a corporal, to receive their rations. We had good coffee morning and night, but had to buy milk, if we had any. The roll-call of the company by the orderly sergeant occurred twice a day, morning and night, and other times when the captain ordered. At dress parade the orderly sergeant had to report to the colonel where every man was, besides sending a written report every day to headquarters at Washington.

The 3d and 4th Maine, the 38th and 40th New York Regiments composed our brigade, and were encamped near each other. Each regiment was a camp by itself, and had a guard around it night and day. Details of soldiers were made every day from each company for guard dnty. They were on guard duty twenty-four hours. The guard was relieved every two hours by a corporal. One dark, stormy night between one and two o'clock, when I was on duty at the guard-house, I was ordered by the officer of the guard to go and see if the men were all at their posts. I had got almost round, when one soldier did not challenge me. "Halt! Who goes there?" "The corporal of the guard with the countersign." "Advance corporal of the guard and give the countersign." This had been gone through with at all other posts, but here I was not challenged. I hunted about where the sentinel ought to be, but could not find him. I went to the officer of the guard and reported one soldier missing from his post. A lieutenant is always officer of the guard, and has command of the guard. The lieutenant told me to get the lantern and we would see if we could find him, — for it was as dark as pitch, and raining fast. We soon found him behind a haystack, fast asleep. The lieutenant waked him up, and asked him if he knew what the consequences were if a soldier was found asleep at his post. He said, he did. An order had lately been issued from headquarters, that a soldier found asleep at his post should be shot. We took him to the guard-house, but I never heard of his case afterwards. I am inclined to think the lieutenant did not report him. In fact I never heard of a soldier being shot for such an offence. The men were not required to work very hard, when they were detailed to work on a fort or at anything else, as a general rule. One day I had charge of a detail of twenty men, two from each company, to cut wood for the regiment. We went three or four miles from camp. The trees had been cut down in the summer, to prevent the rebels from getting near Washington, or the forts without being seen. The trees had to be cut into four feet pieces, and transported to camp by the government teams.

In November our brigade built a theatre. The members of the brigade did all the work, put up the building, made gas to light it, painted the scenery, etc. The men that worked on the building had a free pass to all the plays all winter. Most of the actors were members of the brigade, though two or three stars were usually imported from Washington for the heavy parts. Concerts and plays were given all winter.

One day our regiment had a sham fight. One of Company G, who carried the colors, was badly wounded in the face. Another man who was trying to take the colors accidentally shot him. The wounded man afterwards rejoined the regiment, but carries a big scar on his face to this day from the effects of the sham fight. I saw him at the G A. R. reunion in Boston in 1890. The regiment had no more sham fights after that.

The company used to shoot at a target quite often. The target was shaped like a man, and of about the same size, and was pretty well riddled with bullets by the time we stopped firing. We drilled in the Zouave drill. We used to have drills in the company street quite often among ourselves. A number of men would get together with their muskets, and call on one of the sergeants or corporals to drill them; so we became very proficient in the manual of arms and the company movements by the time we were called upon to fight. The captain used to invite the sergeants and corporals of his company to his tent Sunday afternoons, and give them instructions and good advice. He said he wanted his sergeants and corporals drilled so that they could command the company in case the commissioned officers should be disabled in a fight. He told us to carry some string or small rope and bandages in our pockets to use if we should be wounded. These meetings ended with a concert, there being a number of good singers in the company. Other singers from the rest of the regiment would usually join us after we had commenced singing, so that we had quite a crowd before we left the captain's tent. These meetings were very pleasant as well as instructive.

## CHAPTER X.

### THE PENINSULAR CAMPAIGN.

On the 17th of March, 1862, our division, Hamilton's, afterwards Kearney's, of the 3d corps, Heintzelman's, took the boat for Fortress Monroe, together with the rest of the army. Two or three weeks before we sailed we were ordered to have three days' rations cooked, and to be ready to move at a moment's notice. On our way down the Potomac, we saw Sickles' "Excelsior" brigade encamped on a high bluff on our left. We also passed Mt. Vernon, Washington's old home. It is beautifully situated on high land, about a quarter of a mile back from the river, and commanding a view for a long distance. I counted thirteen steamboats loaded with troops,—all of the 3d corps. On our right, between us and the Virginia shore, five gunboats accompanied us, firing into the woods to dislodge any rebel batteries that might be there. At night we slept in bunks on the steamboat. The orderly sergeant took possession of the best bunk reserved for our company, and kept it for the captain. The Virginia shore for a long distance into the country was covered with woods. On the Maryland shore the ground was more open. Men were ploughing and getting the ground ready to plant. Those on the Maryland shore waved their hats at us as we passed by. We saw the little Monitor some time before we reached our landing place at Fortess Monroe. She looked like a mud-scow with a large cheese box on top, the cheese box representing the turret. As we drew near, at the request of some of the officers, the captain of our transport ship, went very close to the Monitor, so that we had a good chance to see her. A few days before this, the famous fight between the Monitor and Merrimac, had taken place. We could see where the shot had struck the sides and turret of the Monitor. The marks of the shot were about the size of a large saucer. They made dents in the iron of the Monitor, but did not break it, resembling the mark of a musket ball thrown into a piece of putty. The Monitor had steam up, and a naval officer was on top of the turret on the lookout for the Merrimac, expecting another fight.

When we landed at Fortress Monroe, it was raining hard. We marched to our camp ground, and put up our tents; everything was soaking wet. Each soldier was provided with a rubber blanket and a woolen blanket. Two soldiers buttoned their rubber blankets together for a tent. The two blankets were then thrown over a pole or stick, held up by two crotched sticks, about three feet in length, stuck in the ground, six feet apart. The blankets were then fastened down to the ground on each side. One end of the tent was put towards the storm, and covered with a blouse, towel or anything handy. The other end was left open. The tent we happened to have was large enough to hold two men lying down. We put a board down on the ground to keep us out of the water. We put our knapsacks down at the closed end for a pillow, and then put down a woolen blanket to cover the boards. The other woolen blanket we put over us. In fair weather we usually had pine or spruce boughs for a bed. We turned in the first night at Fortress Monroe, with our clothes all on, wet as water could make us, and wrapped ourselves up in our blankets as close as possible. We were warm, and slept well the first night. In the morning, after we got up, our tent smoked like a coal pit. I expected to catch cold, but did not. We felt no bad effects from our exposure. We dried ourselves at a fire made of fence rails, which we found near by.

The 16th Massachusetts was encamped near us. They had been there all winter. Their tents were large Sibly tents, that would hold twenty or thirty. They had a stove in the middle of the tent, and straw to sleep on. They said they had passed a very comfortable winter. General Wood had charge of the department of Fortress Monroe when we arrived there. His orders forbade the soldiers foraging. Our soldiers would get a pig or a hen, when they had a good chance. They acted so badly that an order was issued, confining the soldiers within their regimental lines. Still some had to go out for wood and water, and Mr. Pig would be run within the line. The soldiers inside would kill him as soon as possible, and as a result, we would have roast pig for dinner. One day I saw a pig run inside the lines by a water-carrier. The boys went for him as usual. The pig ran over the tents where some of the soldiers were lying down, and others were writing letters home. He made a great scattering. The soldiers shouted, and there was a great uproar for a while. But we had roast pig for dinner next day, just the same. Some of our company were acquainted with the 16th Massachusetts Regiment, and used to visit them quite often. One day the captain, who wanted to get all the company together for drill, told me to go down to the 16th Massachusetts Regiment with a file of soldiers, and see if I could find several men who were missing. They saw me coming and ran back to camp, reaching there before I did. We did not stay at Fortress Monroe or Hampton very long, and I have no doubt that the inhabitants were glad to get rid of us.

When we began the march, the soldiers threw away great quantities of extra clothing and other things they could possibly spare. I saw one of our company throw into the brush his knapsack and all there was in it. He said he was not going to kill himself lugging around a knapsack. The boys soon got lightened down so that they could march with some comfort. The negroes and poor people had a profitable time in picking up what the soldiers threw away. We passed by Big Bethel where General Butler had been defeated by the rebels the year before. Our troops had some skirmishing with the rebel rear guard, but they soon left us. A few were killed and wounded on both sides. The day we made the final advance on Yorktown, at twelve o'clock, noon, we were eating dinner. We were ordered to march, and had to finish our dinner as we went along. Very soon we were on the double quick. We drove the rebels within the fortifications in a hurry. We passed by a sawmill, not far from the fort, where the rebels had left a pair of horses they had been using to haul logs to the mill, and some cattle they did not have time to get away. The rebels had partly destroyed the saw-mill, but the boys soon repaired it, and went to sawing logs to build houses with. They had one up the next morning.

Now came the siege of Yorktown. We first went into camp in an open field in sight of the rebel fortifications. We soon moved our camp down to the lift in the woods out of sight, where we remained during the siege. We were ordered to move one Sunday. The rain came down in torrents, and we were drenched again. We had to move when ordered, rain or shine. We were engaged in building forts on the right, near the York River. One day we were returning from work in sight of the rebel fortifications, when the enemy fired a solid shot at us from one of their big guns. The ball made such a noise passing over us, that the whole regiment dropped to the ground as if they had been shot. The ball stopped a short distance from us, and after we got to camp, one of the men went back and got it. The next time we went to work we marched round through the woods, so that the rebels couldn't see us. They brobably fired the solid shot to get the range, so as to shell us the next time we came that way.

One time as we were going through another open place on our way to work, we were fired on by the rebel sharp-shooters and cannon. A cannon ball buried itself in a bank on our left. One of the boys went to get the ball. As he was digging with pick and shovel, another ball struck within a foot of him. He dropped his pick and ran for dear life, followed by the shouts and jeers of the whole regiment. We dug for something else besides cannon balls after that.

At another time we were working in a ditch out of sight of the rebels, when a piece of shell struck close by five or six men, but did not hit any of them. Lieutenant Gould had it dug up and sent home. After the close of the war I was in his office on School Street, Boston, one day, and he showed me the piece of shell that came so near killing some of us in the ditch before Yorktown. There were many deaths and many more narrow escapes from death, while we were at work on the fortifications during the siege.

Berdan's sharpshooters were with us while we were at work in the daytime, picking off the rebels with their telescope rifles. Sometimes the boys would put up their hats on their bayonets and let the rebels fire at them. The rebels used to fire their cannon at night, but not so often as in the daytime, our men doing the same.

The soldiers worked on the fortifications day and night. We usually had rations of tobacco and whiskey, when we came in from work. As I did not use either, they were not a great benefit to me. Sometimes I could sell them, but not always, as the soldiers were not very "flush" with money. Sometimes I gave away the tobacco and whiskey; at other times I did not draw them.

During the night of May 3d, we had not heard any firing from the rebel batteries,—a very unusual thing. Our regiment was on picket. At daylight, on the 4th day of May, we heard great cheering in the rebel forts. Our men were in the rebel works. We soon heard that the rebels had left Very soon, three or four men came down where I was; they were all covered with dirt, blood and powder. They had been wounded by torpedoes, found in the ground within the rebel works. A number of our men had been killed by the torpedoes. After that our officers made the rebel prisoners dig up the torpedoes. I soon after went over into the rebel works with the rest of the regiment. The rebels had left large numbers of Sibly tents. The officers' tables were set, with butter, biscuit, and other things, ready for breakfast. Everything looked as if they had left in a hurry.

In one of the streets I found a purse, containing some rebel money, postage stamps, steel pens, and a lock of hair done up in a piece of paper. Soon after the rebels left, a large body of our men went in pursuit. In the afternoon, after marching a few miles from Yorktown, our regiment went into camp. We did not put up our tents, for we expected to march before daylight. In the night it rained. I woke up, and found the rain falling into my face. I pulled my rubber blanket over my head, and went to sleep again. The next day, which was the 5th of May, was cold, and disagreeable. We could hear artillery firing all the forenoon. The battle of Williamsburg had commenced.

We had been supplied with plenty of ammunition before we left Yorktown. In the afternoon we had orders to march. We passed thousands of troops, halting in the fields by the roadside. We asked them if they had been in the fight. They said, "No." Kearney's division had been ordered to the front. We passed lots of artillery, stuck in the mud. The horses were up to their bellies in the mud. The soldiers were all round the cannon, trying to help,—pushing at the wheels, and from behind, and pulling at the tugs; anything to get them out of the mud. We did not stop; we had another job on our hands.

When we were within a mile or two of the battle ground, we were ordered to halt. Our knapsacks, and everything but our rifles, equipments and canteens were left behind, and two men from each company were detailed to guard them. We knew then that we had got to go into the fight. When the detail was made to stay with the equipments, Alexander Greenlough, one of our company, said he had been trying all day to discharge his rifle, but could not, since it had got wet. He asked to be one of the detail to stay with the equipments. The others of his acquaintance made fun of him, and said he was afraid to go into the fight. He said he did not care to stay behind, and would not, if he could help it, since they thought he was a coward, though he said he would be of no use in a battle with a rifle he could not use. He went into the fight, and was the first man in the company to be killed.

The mud stuck to our feet, so that it was difficult walking. One man got into a mud hole, and we had to pull him out. As we came near the battleground we saw General Heintzelman, calling to the soldiers: "No more Bull Runs, men. No more Bull Runs." His staff and a band of music were with him. He called on the band for some music. Everything was said and done to encourage the soldiers and make them do their duty. We could see the rebel fort, Magruder, in the distance. In front of the fort was a plain, this side of the plain was some felled timber, then woods where we were. The rebels were in the felled timber.

Our captain marched the company by the flank. There was a ditch by the side of the road. By stooping down and walking in this ditch we could partly conceal ourselves, as we came into the felled timber. I saw a number of dead and wounded. One wounded man who was sitting behind a log, motioned to me to give him a drink of water. I put the canteen to his mouth, but the poor fellow did not get any water, as the stopper had slipped out on the march. It was a dangerous place for me to stop, and I went on.

We jumped over the logs, shooting at the rebels when we had a chance. I went till I came to a log where one of General Sedgwick's staff was with a number of our men. The rebel balls were flying about them pretty lively. An officer told some of the men to get behind another log. He said we were drawing the rebel fire. Some of the men left. I went where the captain was. We drove the rebels into the fort. As they were going into the fort, I levelled my rifle and gave them a parting salute. After the rebels had got into the fort, they fired shot and shell at us, and kept it up till after dark. The captain could see the flash of the guns, and would shout, "Down." We could get down behind the log before the shell reached us. One of our men was behind a log, raised by two hillocks. His head was too low. A ball struck his head, killing him instantly.

After the rebels had stopped firing, our soldiers began to help the wounded to the rear. When I got up from the ground I could hardly stand. In hurrying into the fight, I had become heated and after lying on the wet ground had become lame and sore. In going to the rear, I met the captain and Corporal Hammond engaged in helping the wounded to the rear. The captain asked me why I was not helping the wounded to the rear. I told him I was so stiff and lame I could hardly walk myself. He told me to go to the rear and warm up. I found a very poor fire, since everything was wet. I managed to beg a cup of coffee from Corporal Shepard. That was all the supper I had that night. For breakfast I had the same as for supper the night before, minus the coffee. Nor did I get a wink of sleep all night. Not daring to lie down on the ground, I stood up behind a tree all night. The rebels evacuated Fort Magruder during the night, and retreated towards Richmond. The next morning it stopped raining. About ten o'clock our cavalry reported the enemy ten miles in advance. We then marched into Williamsburg. I bought some bread, ham and coffee of an old negro, and ate the first square meal I had had for two days, and that wasn't very square. In the afternoon, we went back to get our knapsacks, blankets, etc. We passed over the battle-ground, and had a good opportunity to see the effects of war. It was a sad sight to see so many killed and wounded. I saw one rebel Indian, shot through the forehead. The dead were wrapped up in their blankets and buried together in a shallow trench. I saw one pile of our dead of twenty-nine, packed up against a tree like cord wood, ready for burial. Each company and regiment took care of their wounded, and buried their dead after a battle, if they had time. The ground was so wet that it was difficult to bury the dead out of sight. We buried Alexander Greenlough of our company, near where he fell. The rebel and our dead lay side by side on the battle-ground. There appeared to be as many rebels killed as Union men. We first drove them from the ground. Then they received reinforcements and drove us back. Each side fought over the ground a number of times. At last we drove them into the fort, and they left in the night, as I have stated.

The rebels charged on one of our batteries and took it. But our boys rallied and drove them off before they had time to carry away all the guns. We found our knapsacks all right. We then marched back to Williamsburg, and waited for our train, so as to get three days' rations. When we began a march we were usually provided with three days' rations. The army was in good spirits when the next advance was made. The Army of the Potomac had won its first fight. We stayed a number of days at Williamsburg, getting ready for the next advance.

Williamsburg is a city of ten or twelve thousand inhabitants, and is noted especially for being the seat of William and Mary's College. There were several churches, a large city hall and an insane asylum in the place. We did not see much of the children. I guess they had adjourned the schools. One of the merchants had a lot of rebel money which he invested in tobacco when the rebel army was there. When we took possession of the city, he sold the tobacco to our boys for greenbacks. He evidently thought more of greenbacks than he did of rebel money. He sent to headquarters for a guard for his store, to prevent our troops from stealing his tobacco. We took quite a number of prisoners at Williamsburg. They were put under guard and given rations, the same as our soldiers. Our soldiers gave them tobacco when they asked for it. I heard one prisoner say his home was in Alexandria, and that he would stay there if he ever got back there again. Many rebels stayed in the woods away from their army, and gave themselves up when we arrived. When we left the city, I saw quite a number of ladies wave their handkerchiefs at us. I am inclined to think there were Union people there. After leaving Williamsburg we found the roads so soft in some places that we had to put logs down to enable the teams to pass along. These were called corduroy roads. In many places the roads were obstructed with trees, which the rebels had felled.

One day when we did not march, Corporal Shepard and I went some distance from camp to wash some clothes. We were about half through with our washing, when we heard the assembly sound for drill. When we arrived at camp, the orderly sergeant wanted to know if we had been on drill. We told him "No." He said the colonel had ordered us under arrest for being absent from drill. We told Lieutenant Gould we were out washing some clothes, and did not get back in season. He went to see the colonel to get our release, which he refused to give. The lieutenant told us we might go and see the colonel, but he thought it would be of no use. I went to the colonel and told him I had never been off duty before since I had joined the regiment. He still refused to let us off, and said we must take the consequences. We were ordered to our tent and were not allowed to leave, and a guard was put over us. The guard was soon taken off,—and this was in our favor. When we resumed the march we were given our old places in the company. That ended our case. I had tented with Shepard all the time we had been on the Peninsular. I noticed that the others changed tent-mates nearly every night, and finally told Shepard I thought we ought to change, also. He assented. I do not think, however, I gained any advantage by the change.

On the march we usually halted for the night before sundown. One day, late in the afternoon, we halted for the night as usual. I was gathering some pine boughs for a bed, while my tent-mate was getting supper, when we heard the assembly. We knew we had got to march. There was much grumbling and not a little profanity, for we did not like to be deprived of our sleep. We marched all night among the army wagons. The rebel cavalry were hovering round, intending to destroy our wagon-trains, if they had a good opportunity. It was a very pleasant night, and the moon shone all night.

Arriving at White House, on the Pamunkey River, we were encamped there several days. The steamers came up the river from Washington with supplies for the army. Some of the boats had things to sell the soldiers. I bought a loaf of white bread, which was a great treat. From White House we marched towards Richmond. At the time of the battle of Fair Oaks we had just received three days' rations. In the forenoon we heard more firing than usual. Lieutenant Gould, who had charge of the company, told me to take my place as sergeant after that. Captain Ingalls had been promoted major, after the battle of Williamsburg.

Before noon, General Kearney rode by with his staff. As soon as the soldiers saw him, they said we should have to fight again before long. He inquired of some of the men what regiment they belonged to. They told him the 40th New York. He said, "Very well, very well," and rode on. He used to talk with the soldiers quite often, especially when there was going to be a fight. We saw an orderly ride up to the colonel's tent shortly after, and deliver a message. Our regiment was then ordered into line. General Casey's division of 12,000 or 15,000 men who were in advance, were being driven back, and our corps, who were on the reserve, were ordered up to stop the rebel advance. Casey's men were going to the rear in squads, captains with parts of their companies, and colonels with parts of their regiments, in full retreat. I saw one captain with a musket in his hand. He had been fighting with his men. The right and left companies of our regiment were ordered to support Randolph's Rhode Island Battery. Our company was one of the two. In front of the battery were some earthworks. In our front was an open plain, and then woods. On our left and rear were thirty-six pieces of artillery, to sweep the plain in front. In the woods on our right was the infantry. The two companies were divided into squads of four men each. The best marksman was to fire, while the other three loaded. No man was permitted to leave the ranks for any cause, and as a result we had to go without supper and breakfast again. At night, the rebel line was close to ours. The 3d corps checked the advance of the enemy in the afternoon. I saw General Heintzelmans in company with a colonel and part of his regiment, come out of the woods in our front in retreat behind his batteries. But he had stopped the rebel advance. He said he would have some of their batteries before night. Our officers were at work all night, perfecting the line of battle for the coming fight. In the night we heard a noise on the plain in our front. The long roll was beat, and every one was on the alert. An officer came from the other part of the line, and wanted to know what that noise was. A horse had got loose, and was running about over the plan. After it was known what made the noise, everything was quiet again. We thought the rebels were coming to attack us, sure. We did not get much sleep that night. The rebel general expected to drive the 3d corps as he had driven Casey's division. In that he was mistaken. At daylight the two lines of battle commenced firing. It was the loudest firing I ever heard, and extended all along the line.

General Heintzelman's headquarters were on our left and rear, under a large tree, and we had a good chance to see how a fight was conducted. He sent off a great many orders by his staff and orderlies; some were verbal, and some were in writing, such as, "Tell General Sedgwick to be sure and keep the connection." I saw General Kearney come in from the fight. His horse was so tired he could hardly go. He had a number of horses at General Heintzelman's headquarters. He could not mount a horse without help, having lost an arm in the Mexican war. He stopped to talk a few moments with General Heintzelman, then mounted another horse, and away he went again. After awhile we could hear loud cheering up in the woods on our right. Our troops were driving the enemy. General Heintzelman climbed up on the bank, swung his hat, and called for three cheers. "Those are our boys. Give them three cheers." Everybody cheered as loud as he could. He was so excited, he could hardly stand still. General Hooker was sent in over the plain on our left with part of his division to flank the rebels. After he had got started, General Heintzelman sent a staff officer after him with some message. The staff officer rode like the wind. General Hooker got in the rear of the enemy, and then the rebel prisoners came in. They were the "Home Guard," composed of rich men's sons from Richmond. They wore fine gray uniforms.

Our soldiers captured a large four-horse coach from Richmond. It was marked Spotwood Hotel, and was filled with planters, who had come from Richmond to see the fight. They had a negro driver. The soldiers told the planters they wanted the coach, and informed the negro that they would dispense with his services, as they could drive themselves. I heard loud cheering in our front, and did not know what to make of it. Soon I saw the four-horse coach coming. It was covered with soldiers inside and out. They were on top, on the brake, and on behind where the baggage is carried. They were cheering, and having a great time. The coach was afterwards used to carry off our wounded. The rebel prisoners were very crestfallen; they did not look up very often, they felt so badly. They had expected to drive us into the Chickahominy, instead of being captured. Our men treated them well. I told some of Casey's men that our boys had driven the rebels back where they came from. They said they did not believe it. It was Casey's men that had been repulsed the day before. Late in the afternoon we were allowed to get something to eat. Casey's men had gone through our camp and taken our three days' rations, so that we could not find anything to eat. I went to our commissary department, and said I wanted three days' rations, and got them. One of Casey's division told me that our men fought well, but the rebels were all around them before they knew it.

General McClellan came to General Heintzelman's headquarters late in the afternoon, to see how he was getting along. I saw General McClellan when he came in our neighborhood; he rode a few paces ahead of his body guard. Seeing a soldier with his arm done up in a sling, he stopped and asked him if he was much hurt and then rode on. Arriving at General Heintzelman's headquarters, he shook hands with the leading generals who had been in the fight, and some others,—Heintzelman, Kearney, Hooker, Sedgwick; all had a pleasant smile on their faces. General Heintzelman knelt down on one knee, and marked out on the ground how he won the fight. The others stood round him in a circle. When he was telling of some important movement, he would look up to McClellan, who would nod his head and smile. It was a great sight to see so many distinguished generals together at one time. They appeared to enjoy one another's company. General McClellan's headquarters were about fifteen miles nearer Richmond than we were at the time of the battle of Fair Oaks. We were on the left wing of the army. It took a couple of days to get settled down to camp-life again after the fight; the dead had to be buried, and the wounded to be provided for.

At the time when a general advance was ordered along the whole line at the battle of Fair Oaks, our regiment had to charge across an open plain before they could get at the rebels in the woods, and many were shot down. The color guard of our regiment, consisting of twelve men, were all killed or wounded. One of the color sergeants was wounded in the thumb; five balls had passed through his clothes and hat. Corporal Braslin, the color guard from our company, was dangerously wounded in the hip. Some of our boys carried him to the railroad station, where he took the train for White House. From there he was transported to Annapolis in a steamboat, and placed in the hospital. Some of our boys, who carried him to the station, said he would never live to get to Annapolis. He got better, obtained a furlough, and returned to Arlington. On one occasion he made some remarks at a public meeting there. He said he was going back to the front. They passed round the hat, and got eighty dollars for him. He served out his time in the army, and was present at one of our reunions not long since.

When the color guard is formed, the colonel sends to the captain of each company in the regiment for a soldier for color guard. Captain Ingalls sent Corporal Braslin. There are also two color sergeants, making twelve in all. The color guard have no fatigue, picket, guard or other duties to perform. They are with the colors all the time. They are placed in the centre of the regiment on dress parade and in the line of battle.

And now came camp life again, with its picket and fatigue duty, and drilling in company and battalion movements, when we had nothing else to do. One night a part of our company was on the reserve picket. In the morning, Lieutenant Gould was ordered to take four of his men and scout outside of the picket line. He was told to be careful, and not to go too far until he knew his country, so as to avoid a surprise. He passed the outside picket post, which was in charge of Sergeant Floyd of our company. He had gone but a short distance, when he was fired on by some rebels from behind a log. Two of his men fell, Thompson and Ellis. The rest returned the fire, and retreated to the reserve picket. Before they retreated, Lieutenant Gould unbuckled his sword and placed it on the fallen bodies of his men. The reserve picket heard the firing, and were in line when the lieutenant came back. The officer of the picket told him to take his company and secure the bodies of his men that had been shot. It was in the woods where they had been killed, and the underbrush was very thick. The lieutenant deployed his company on the right of the road and ordered them to advance. The men next to the road were fired on by some rebel cavalrymen. We were then ordered to halt and afterwards to retreat, without recovering the bodies of Thompson and Ellis. One of the scouts afterwards recovered Ellis' body, and it was buried at Fair Oaks. Thompson and Ellis had come from Arlington with us, and Lieutenant Gould and all the rest of us felt very sorry to lose them. Lieutenant Gould was afterwards put under arrest, but none of us thought he was to blame. It was one of the casualties of war. He never recovered his sword and belt. The company made him a present of another one, costing thirty-five dollars. He was very popular with the men. Lieutenant Graves presented him with the sword and belt in behalf of the company, in a neat speech. Lieutenant Gould's complimentary reply was cheered heartily by the company. When we marched again, Lieutenant Gould was released, and placed in command of the company.

## CHAPTER XI.

### THE SEVEN DAYS' FIGHT.

And now we come to the Seven Days' Fight, and the retreat to the James River. Before the retreat commenced a general order from General Kearney was read to the regiment by the colonel. The officers and men were ordered to destroy all their private property. The men were ordered to put eighty rounds of cartridges in their knapsacks, besides the usual forty rounds in our cartridge box, and nothing but hard bread in our haversacks. When the men were fighting, the officers were cautioned to have everybody in his place and doing his duty. On the charge the officers were ordered to take the lead.

One night our regiment was on picket duty in front of our intrenchments, in a piece of woods, where there were some earthworks, about two feet in height. The rebels were very near us all night, so that we could hear them talk. They commenced firing on both sides in the night. It was as dark as dark could be. Which side commenced the firing, I I do not know. There was nothing to fire at, for we could not see anything. The officers on both sides ordered the men to stop firing. I did not fire, but was ready to kill the first man who came over the earthworks. After awhile the firing ceased, and everything was quiet for the rest of the night· But I did not sleep any all night, and I do not think many did on that picket line. A short time before daylight we retreated out of the woods. General Kearney was between us and the rebels. I heard the ball go whizzing by that was intended to kill him, fired by one of the rebel skirmishers. At another time, before we retreated, we were driven inside the intrenchments. We then went above the enemy on the double-quick, and tried to get in their rear. The rebels saw what we were up to, and ran like good fellows, and as they ran faster than we did, managed to escape us. We could hear heavy firing on our right, where General McClellan was two or three days before we retreated. The day before we retreated, we were given two months' pay. I went to Major Ingalls' tent, our old captain, to get him to sign some papers, so that I could send the money home. I asked him if the fight was in our favor, and he said it was not. He said it would be hard telling who would come out of the fight alive. That was the last time I ever saw him to speak with him. He was wounded in the leg at Charles City Cross Roads in the Seven Days' Fight. His leg was amputated in hospital at Annapolis, Maryland, but he died shortly after from the effects of the wound. He left a wife and child at Arlington. They came out to see him, and stayed a number of days, when we were at Camp Sacket, in the fall of 1861.

On the fourth day we retreated to a place near Savage Station. All of the three days we could hear heavy firing on our right and rear. Near the station we could see carloads of ammunition blown up to prevent them from falling into the hands of the enemy. For they had cut the railroad between White House and Savage Station. In our rear where we had come from, we could see coming over the hill, artillery and parts of artillery, fleeing from the enemy as fast as they could go. The teamsters were lashing the horses to make them go faster. There was a large body of cavalry near where we were, which was ordered by General Heintzelman to go to the defence of the batteries. He went with them. He wore a blouse and a felt hat, so that he could not be recognized by the enemy. It was a great sight to see such a large body of cavalry and artillery going at such a frightful rate. The ground fairly trembled with the shock. I never saw such a sight, before nor since, in horseflesh. In a retreat the officers have to be in the rear to see what is going on. Very soon we were ordered to march down the road where the artillery went. Some more batteries tore past us as we were in the road. Our men heard them coming, and shouted out, "Right and left, right and left," so that we stepped both sides of the road to let them go by, and nobody was hurt. It was a very warm day in June, and my load of cartridges was becoming very tiresome. I stepped out of the ranks and pulled the tins out of my cartridge-box, and packed it solid with cartridges,—eighty rounds, twice as many as I could get in with the tins in. In the tins of a cartridge-box there are forty cells, one for each cartridge. I left my knapsack with the rest of the cartridges in the bush. I could then march with some comfort. I saved a few sheets of paper, envelopes, postage stamps and a lead pencil, so that I could write home. Late in the afternoon we reached a bridge that was being built. The timbers were in place, but no plank. We marched over the creek on the timbers. After we had crossed, our skirmishers commenced firing. The enemy were in our front. We were not expecting to find them there. General Kearney was in the rear. Hearing the firing, he came where we were. He ran his horse through the creek. He was all covered with mud and water. He found General Birney, who commanded the brigade, and ordered him to march three of the regiments back over the bridge as quickly as possible, while he took the fourth regiment and engaged the enemy. After Birney got the three regiments back across the bridge, Kearney joined him with the fourth. We then proceeded by another road. It was a narrow escape, for if the enemy had attacked us at the right time with infantry and artillery, they might have killed or captured the whole brigade. So much for having a good officer to command our division. We marched until late at night, and had some supper of hard bread and coffee without any milk. The milkman didn't come round during the Seven Days' Fight.

The next morning we ate our breakfast, and had everything ready to march before daylight. The first person I heard in the morning was General Kearney, waking up his staff and orderlies. He told them, "Wake up. We must be after the enemy." We marched a short distance and formed in line of battle on the edge of an open field, and waited for the enemy. There were lots of blackberries a short distance in our rear, and some of the men left the ranks to gather them. The officers told them they must not go far, and to come back as soon as they heard the drums. I went with the rest, and picked a good quantity of berries. Soon we heard the drums beat, and the men ran to get into their places. We were soon enough, for the rebels did not attack us for fifteen or twenty minutes. When our skirmishers were driven in, we moved down to the left into some woods and felled timber. Randolph's Battery came along where we were, in a hurry. They couldn't get through on account of the felled timber. They had just lost one of their guns, the rebels having shot one of the wheel horses. They cut the harnesses from the dead horse and the other wheel horses, and left in a hurry, abandoning the cannon. I saw by the looks of the drivers of the battery and the officers, that something disagreeable had happened. Late in the afternoon we got out of water. It was very warm, and we were very thirsty. Two men were detailed from our company with twelve canteens each to get some water. They returned without any. Two more were sent out afterwards, with the same result. In the afternoon we were moved further to the left, near where there was some hard fighting. Shells were flying about in a most lively fashion, and one piece came near Kearney's horse. The soldiers dodged behind trees to get out of the way of the shells. Kearney said to them, "Those shells don't hurt me. They won't hurt you."

Our skirmishers were moved forward two or three times in the afternoon, and found the enemy in heavy force in our front. Heavy fighting continued all the afternoon on our left. This was the battle of Charles City Cross Roads, fought the day before we reached Malvern Hill. At night we posted our pickets. Oh! for a drink of water. Late in the night the pickets were taken away. The officers went along the line and whispered to the men, so that the rebels would not know when we left. Oh! for a drink of water. We marched the rest of the night without getting any. One time I thought I was going to get some. I saw a wet place in the road, and scooped the water up in my hand. But it was mud, water and sand, and I had to spit it out. We came to Malvern Hill about daylight. Soon after some of our men said there was plenty of water about twenty rods down to the left. I ran to the water and drank my fill. I expected to feel some bad effects from drinking so much, but did not. I filled my canteen and dipper, for fear I should get out again. There were many soldiers at the spring for water. As I was returning to my regiment, I met a man who wanted to know if I could give him a drink. I told him there was plenty a short distance down the hill. He was so thirsty that I gave him what I had in my dipper. I was very tired and sleepy, and one of my feet was sore. We had marched all night, without sleep or water. I went a short distance and sat down. Another regiment came where I was, and I thought they were going to walk over me. The colonel wanted to know if I was wounded, and I told him, "Yes."

After resting a little while, I started to find my regiment. I found them in company with Randolph's Battery of five guns, one having been lost the day before, as I have stated. Our regiment was detailed to support this battery in the battle of Malvern Hill. The battery was placed near the foot of the hill. Back of us, about half way up the hill, was the hospital belonging to the regiment, with its red flag flying. In our front was a small brook. The ground was low and marshy. Beyond that was a hill, wooded on top. On our left was some brush, with woods beyond. Our regiment was posted on the right, and in front of the battery. Some of the men had to lie down when the guns were fired. We had picks and shovels, and went to work constructing earthworks. A man on horseback rode out on the hill in our front, and after a short time rode back again. We thought it was General Lee, but I did not see anyone fire at him. About nine o'clock a rebel battery came out of the woods on top of the hill in front, and commenced firing at us. Our battery fired in return. We were ready and waiting for them. The men "went at it" in a lively manner. Our men had their coats off and their sleeves rolled up above their elbows. Every man connected with the battery worked with a will. The balls from the enemy came thick and fast. The captain of the battery rode back and forth in the rear of the guns, encouraging the men, saying, "Give it to 'em. Let 'em have it." One of the corporals who had charge of the gun nearest to us, told the captain that he had no water to wet the sponge to cool the gun with. The captain said, "Give it to them without water." One of the shells burst just as it left the gun and hit one of our men. The soldiers began to go to the rear, saying they were not going to be shot by their own men. But we had to stay where we were.

Three men near me were hit by the enemy's shells during the fight. Gleason, one of our company, was behind a bundle of straw. A shell struck him, and threw him, straw and all, three or four rods in the rear. The shot made a bad wound in his back, and he died soon after he reached the hospital. Another man named Thompson, one of the oldest men in the company, was wounded. He was not further than three or four feet from me, when he was struck.

Another man of our regiment, but not of our company, was wounded in the head by a piece of shell. He lay insensible for three days. He was taken to the hospital at Hampton, Va., where he recovered. He was afterwards present at the battle of Gettysburg. Our colonel had orders to report at Gettysburg at a certain time. He sent word he would be there if he did not have five men. He told the regiment to keep up with him, if possible, but if they could not, to get there as soon as they could. He arrived on time, but had only seventeen of the regiment with him. George Harrington was one of the seventeen. He is now postmaster at East Boston, and as jovial as ever. Our regiment lost one hundred and fifty men at Gettysburg; but I am getting a head of my story. There were many killed and wounded from our regiment at the battle of Malvern Hill, but how many I have not the means of knowing. At one time the captain of the battery, seeing a shell burst under the rebel guns, told the gunner to give them a solid shot. The solid shot hit on the axle of a rebel gun and knocked it to pieces. The corporal who fired the shot, climbed on the gun, took off his hat and gave three cheers. It was a chance shot, but it did the work, just the same. When the captain had seen the effects of the solid shot, he rode away to see some of the other gunners. One of the lieutenants told the captain they were out of spherical shot. The captain sent a man on horseback over the hill to the rear where the reserve ammunition was kept. He came back with a four-horse load. The battery took a supply, and away went the four-horse wagon back over the hill on the double-quick.

The gunners were fortunate in not being disabled during the engagement. I did not see any men or horses hit during the day. In action the horses are placed in the rear of the guns, facing the enemy. But there were many narrow escapes. I saw a solid shot strike between the fore legs of one of the lead horses, and run under the six horses and the caisson, rolling up the hill a quarter of a mile away. The horse hopped up on all fours, pawed the ground, shook his head, snorted, and appeared to be greatly excited, but he made no attempt to run away. The horses appeared to know what was going on as well as the men.

We expected the rebel infantry would attack the battery during the afternoon, but they did not come. At one time General Kearney told the colonel that the rebels would make us a visit in about five minutes. We examined our rifles to see if they were all right. Later the general told the colonel they would pay us a visit in about three minutes. But they would have to drive back our regiment before they could reach the battery, and that would be a difficult thing to do, unless they attacked us in superior force. For the 40th New York had a good reputation for fighting, and our colonel, E. W. Egan, was a fighting man. He was afterwards promoted major-general.

Our battery could not silence the rebel battery. Another battery of four twelve-pound howitzers came into position on our left, about the middle of the afternoon. The rebel battery left, and we were glad of it. Late in the afternoon, we saw some men on horseback on the top of the hill in our rear. We were told by a man who came from the hospital that it was General McClellan and his staff.

The great charge of the day was made near us on our left. I heard a loud noise behind me. Looking back I saw the hill all covered with troops, artillery, cavalry and infantry, all on the double-quick. They were hurrying to reinforce the left, when the great charge was made by Stonewall Jackson. We could hear the grape and canister fired by our batteries, crash into the brush. The attack was repulsed with great loss to the enemy, and the Army of the Potomac was saved.

After dark our regiment moved back over the top of the hill, when we came to a halt and commenced throwing up earthworks, expecting to fight there the next day. I was so tired that I went to sleep standing, after we halted. I had a detail of men to look after, that were at work on the earthworks. Lieutenant Gould told me to keep them at work. I thought I could look after them as well sitting down as standing; but as soon as I touched the ground I was fast asleep again, though I had no intention of going to sleep. The lieutenant came along and hit me with the flat of his sword, and said, "Fletcher, this won't do." I did not allow myself to lie down again, but kept walking about during the whole night. Next morning we started for Harrison's Landing, arriving there in the afternoon. It rained most of the day. There was a large field of wheat near where we were stationed. It was done up in shocks, but the cavalry had taken most of it for their horses. I managed to get some loose straw, but as it was soaking wet, it wasn't of much use. I wanted it for a bed

After we arrived at the landing, Corporal Hammond, my old chum, gave out. He sat down under a tree, and would not stir. Shepard and I pitched a tent and built up a fire. We then dragged Hammond into the tent by main force; he was so exhausted that he could not help himself. We gave him some hot coffee and made him as comfortable as possible for the night. He afterwards was taken to the hospital and narrowly escaped dying. He joined the regiment sometime later, and served in the Wilderness campaign.

After our arrival at Harrison's Landing, there was some confusion in the army, as there always is after a big fight. I was sergeant of the guard the night following our arrival. I was all right, but somewhat tired and sleepy. I could have fought the next day on a pinch, however, but many could not. The next morning General Kearney drove in some cows, so as to have some milk for his hospital. We went into camp in the woods, and constructed some earthworks near by. One night our regiment was in the earthworks all night, expecting an attack, but the rebels did not come. We soon settled down to camp life again.

One day, General McClellan, the President, and other dignitaries made us a visit. One night about twelve o'clock, without any warning, we heard heavy artillery firing in the direction of the river. The long roll was beat, and all the troops got into line in a hurry. No one knew what the firing was for. Men were sent to the river to find out. On their return, they reported that the rebels were firing into our boats on the river. Our gunboats soon silenced the enemy, and we went to sleep again. The next day "Little Mac" sent some troops over the river and kept them there, so that we had no further trouble from that quarter.

During the Seven Days' Fight I had lost and destroyed many things that a soldier wants, but which the government does not provide. So I wrote to my sister to send me a box of such things. The box was sent, but I never received it. It came to Harrison's Landing, after we had marched, followed me to Alexandria and to Centreville and below, when we went to reinforce General Pope; then back again to Alexandria, up to Harper's Ferry, in fact it followed the regiment wherever it went. Some of the boys got it after I had lost my leg, and thinking I would never want it again, divided the contents among themselves.

One night, when I was on picket at Harrison's Landing, I had to take a piece of phosphorus wood to see what time it was, to relieve the guard. I could see quite plainly, by holding a piece of this wood close to the watch. There were large quantities of phosphorus in the Virginia woods. We were not allowed to make a fire or light a match, for fear of being seen by the enemy. I was sergeant of the guard, and Lieutenant Gould was officer of the guard. I tented with him that night. We talked a large part of the night about home, where we had been to school, and what we had done after leaving school. It appeared that he had been to Westford Academy where I had attended school. We did not see any rebels that night, but they were so near that we were cautioned not to make any unnecessary noise.

Soon after arriving at the Landing we were ordered on fatigue duty. Only a small number reported for duty. The officer who had charge of the fatigue party, wanted to know where the men were. He was told that they were sick and lame. He ordered the sick and lame on duty. I had a lame foot, but was compelled to go with the rest of the cripples. We did not do much work. Some had their heads done up in a handkerchief, others their arms in a sling; and we were a sorry looking set, generally. Much of the sickness and lameness was feigned; we appeared as lame and sick as possible. The rest of the regiment laughed at us when we came to where they were. Nearly every body felt miserable for a number of days after the Seven Days' battle. But the wood had to be cut down, and fortifications had to be constructed to protect us from the enemy.

One day, in company with another soldier, I obtained a pass to go down to the Landing, about three miles distant, to see the place, and find out what was going on. We thought we saw an opportunity to make a little money to replenish our purses, which were getting low, by buying things of the steamboats that came up the river from Washington, and selling them to the soldiers about the Landing. I had five dollars, and the other man had twenty-five dollars. We bought twelve bottles of honey, canned meats and other things. For the honey we paid fifteen dollars for twelve bottles, and sold it for two dollars a bottle. From the other things we bought, we cleared a handsome sum. In two or three hours we made twenty dollars. My partner furnished most of the money, but I did most of the trading. He thought he ought to have fifteen dollars, which left me only five dollars. We had nearly sold out, when we found out that we were disobeying the rules by selling to the soldiers. The provost marshal made his appearance, and we left for camp in a hurry.

## CHAPTER XII.

### SECOND BULL RUN AND CHANTILLY.

In August we were on the march again. We were ordered to put every ounce we could spare into our knapsacks, which would be sent to us by boat. I put in my knapsack my testament which had been given me at Arlington, intending to bring it home with me when I came, my pistol, and in fact all my private property. My revolver cost fifteen collars. I never saw the knapsack or any of its contents again. I heard later that the rebels sunk the boat which carried our knapsacks in the James River. So I suppose my knapsack is at the bottom of the James.

Our first day's march was quite rapid, and I was tired when night came. The regiment encamped in line of battle near a farm house. After breaking ranks the men ran for the tobacco house first of all, and filled their haversacks with tobacco. I managed to secure five or six sweet potatoes about as big as my little finger. I boiled them in my dipper, and thought they were the best sweet potatoes I ever ate. I saw some cotton growing in the garden for the first time. It looked very beautiful. It was planted in rows three feet apart, and was twelve or fifteen inches high.

That night as General Kearney was examining the roads, he was approached by a man who told him his soldiers were stealing horses out of the man's barn. "I don't want to know anything about your horses. I want to know where this road goes to," replied the General.

The next morning we started in good season, and had another forced march. At night we encamped near a corn field. The corn was just right to roast, which was a great treat to us. I had to go quite a distance into the field before I could get a supply; the boys had evidently been there before. While getting my corn, I heard considerable noise in front, like some one running towards me. I thought the rebels wene coming. Soon I saw a hen running, pursued by one of our soldiers. They did not see me. I suppose one fellow had chicken for supper that night.

When we left next morning, there was very little corn left in the field. The soldiers took everything about the place that was fit to eat. When we left Harrison's Landing we took a little bag of salt, which we obtained of the cook. The salt worked in well here with the parched corn. Blackberries were plenty, but we did not have much time to pick them.

In the morning we took an early start, and hurried forward again. At night we encamped near a grocery store. The soldiers found a pair of mules in the cellar and two or three barrels of cider. "Pass your dippers round, boys," and away went the cider. The doors and windows of the grocery store were all nailed up; so the boys thought there must be something good inside. It did not take long to open the doors, and lots of good things were found inside,— sugar, molasses, tea, coffee, and other good things which we helped ourselves to. One of the boys handed me a pint of sugar, which I managed to get rid of. The boys took everything they could find that was good to eat, and nobody tried to stop them. In the house near by were a man and some women, but they never said a word. I learned afterwards that the man who owned the store traded with the union scouts when they came there, and with the rebel scouts and pickets when they came round. We had just come from the Seven Days' fight, and thought we had already paid the the rebels for anything we might take.

When we arrived at Yorktown, we found the three months' men guarding the place. They were dressed up in nice clean clothes, with shoes blacked, and wearing white gloves. Quite a contrast to us who had gone through the Peninsular Campaign, with our ragged and dirty clothes. The boys made lots of fun of them. " Say, mister, what was the price of white gloves in New York, when you left," called out one of our boys to a "dudish" looking sentinel.

As soon as we arrived at Yorktown, our regiment embarked on a steamer and sailed to Alexandria, where we stopped only a few hours. No one was allowed to leave the ranks. How I wished I had a little money to buy something nice to eat! A dollar even would be a great relief. One of the lieutenants owed me twenty-five cents, which I tried to get, but could not, for he was out of money. Every one was out of money.

At Alexandria we took the cars to reinforce Gen. Pope. We went about twenty-five miles south of Centreville towards Richmond, riding part of the way on the cars, and marching part of the way. We could hear the sound of war again, —artillery in the distance.

The negroes were going to the rear in large numbers. I saw one old negro driving a pair of very fat oxen, which were yoked to a long wagon, and in the wagon were lots of little negroes, too small to walk. As he passed by us he called out: "Jackson too much for d'em, Jackson too much for d'em," then he would whip up the oxen. There were not many in the crowd but old men and women and little children.

We hunted and hunted for water fit to drink, but could not find any. It was of a reddish color and did not taste good. I did not like the looks of the country here, and would much prefer to live on the peninsular between the York and James Rivers.

The first thing we knew the whole rebel army was in our rear, and we went back after them by forced marches. We marched till late at night. At last I told Sergeant Wiley, one of our men, that I was not going any further that night, rebels or no rebels. He said he felt about as I did, and we commenced to get supper of salt beef, hard bread and coffee. The regiment did not go much further, and we went up to where they camped. Other regiments were encamped all about us. Far and wide we could see their camp fires. We could see the fires at Centreville that the rebels had started. They destroyed large quantities of military stores and long trains of cars full of supplies for our army.

The next morning one whole regiment was deployed across the railroad track as skirmishers, but we did not see the enemy. Many houses were full of wounded soldiers from Joe Hooker's Fight, as he came down to reinforce General Pope.

We found Centreville still burning, as well as our supplies. We drove the enemy from Centreville before they had time to remove or destroy all the goods. I saw large quantities of shoes, beef, hard bread, pork and other things. I stopped to pick up a piece of pork and hard bread. The bread was much better than what I had, so I emptied my haversack, and filled it with good bread.

The rebels burned the bridge below Centreville, thereby preventing teams from going to Washington. After we drove the rebels from Centreville, they returned to their old battle ground at Bull Run. I saw General Pope and staff when they arrived at Centreville. As he came in sight, General Kearney rode down to meet him, and asked if he should put his cavalry in advance. General Pope said, "No, I want General Burnside to get to a certain place before you start." General Kearney was very indignant, and came back twitching his horse's rein impatiently, with his one arm. This was about twelve o'clock.

If General Kearney had had his say, he would have had a lively fight with them that afternoon, but as it was, the rebel army had all that afternoon to get in good position and already for us the next morning.

We moved towards Bull Run and our regiment formed a hollow square ready to receive cavalry, the other regiments doing the same. The distance between us was ten or fifteen rods. Our cavalry took prisoners of one picket post of fifteen or twenty men, but when they made a second charge they were repulsed. We saw them come out of the woods after their defeat. Some afoot, some horses were without riders, some soldiers were wounded and hardly able to cling to their horses, and the others scattered all about the country. A cavalry repulse is an awful sight to see.

That night we camped where we were. After breakfast the next morning three days' rations were issued, also forty rounds of cartridge to each man, cap box replenished, and the sergeant inspected each man's cap and cartridge box to be sure he was supplied. We were also marched to a stream of water to fill our canteens. Everyone looked sober, and very little talking was done. The soldiers know when they are going into a fight. We could hear the artillery in front. Batteries passed us going to the front covered with hay, the horses with bags of oats on their backs.

Everything pointed towards a big fight. The rebels were in heavy force in a piece of woods on an open plain, in our front. Our army tried all the morning to get the rebels out of those woods, but in vain. General Kearney was to try his hand; he sent our brigade—Birney's—four regiments on the right of the woods to flank them. When we came to the hill, we were shelled from the confederate artillery. The shells came thick and fast. One piece touched the hair on the back of my head and dropped at my heels. I was stunned, for an instant, but only a moment.

Then came the order from General Birney: "By the left flank, march, double quick, march." We were coming on the rear of the rebels in that piece of woods. The enemy ran up the hill firing at us as they went. Then came the order from Birney: "Fire!" and we did it, loading and firing as fast as we could. When I saw a man, I fired at him, but

I fired just the same if I could see no one. The order always was obeyed. I saw that one of our men, named Booth, was shot in the leg. After we had driven the enemy up the hill I asked Lieutenant Gould if I could go back and get Booth. The orders were not to have any man leave the ranks, he said. As we were not firing, I thought I should have time to go back before the order came to advance. Booth lay there for a week with scarcely anything to eat. He was nothing but a skeleton when found. One of the Sanitary Commission found him and brought him to Washington. After the retreat of our army, some of the rebels who came along would give him something to eat, and others take it away.

Late in the afternoon we drove the enemy out of another piece of woods. They were down in an old railroad cut. We had expended most of our forty rounds before we got them out, but they had to go. Down in the cut we went after them, over the cut, and up the other side. I stopped in the cut to fire at a rebel who had just left; he was not more than four or five rods from me. I supposed I could drop him without any difficulty. I fired, but he didn't stop. I was excited and too sure of my mark.

After crossing the bank on the other side, we found the enemy's dead very numerous. I saw several rebels lying down in a ditch or low place with their faces to the ground. They were undoubtedly alive. I asked them what they were lying down there for; but they did not answer. I was very busy firing at the time, and did not molest them.

At last we began to get short of ammunition, and some of the soldiers were all out, and were taking cartridges from those that had fallen. After we had gone a little distance from the cut, I saw the regiment going to the rear. I knew they had orders to retreat, though I did not hear the order, for they were all going together. I started to go with them One Lieutenant M., of another company in our regiment, said: "Hold on. They'll be back here in a minute," at the same time swinging his sword in the air, and calling, "Come on, boys." Supposing he knew what the order was, I kept on firing, for I had a few more cartridges left. He was shot through the body. The rebels were in heavy force in our front in plain sight. Not liking to be so much exposed, I stepped a few feet to the right, and kept on firing through a crotched tree. I was now getting out of cartridges. Looking around me, I saw none of the regiment in sight. I felt sure the rebels knew where I was, because I could hear the balls strike the tree or whizz by, when I exposed any part of my body. What to do I did not know. To run to the rear seemed certain death, and to be taken prisoner was about as bad. I grasped my musket, and ran to the rear as fast as my legs would carry me. The rebel balls flew around me like hailstones, but not one touched me. It seemed almost a miracle that I was not hit. I did not have to go very far, as it was in the woods, though the trees were not very thick. I had gone but a few rods to the rear, when I came to Lieutenant M., who had been mortally wounded in the body. Lieutenant Fletcher of Co. G., his intimate friend, was with him, and one or two others. He was in great pain. They asked me for water, and I gave them all I had in my canteen. I took his equipments and the others carried him till we came to an ambulance. He begged Lieutenant Fletcher not to leave him. Fletcher said he would not, though he was disobeying orders in being away from his company. Fletcher asked me to find his captain, Lindsay, and tell him where he was, but to tell no other living man.

I saw another wounded man near the ambulance. One of his heels had been cut off by a piece of shell, as clean as if cut by a knife.

After seeing Lieutenant M. in the ambulance, I looked around to find my regiment. It was getting dark. I inquired of everybody I saw if they knew where the 40th New York or Birney's brigade was. Nobody seemed to know. It was now so dark that I could hardly see. At last I saw a fire a short distance away. I went to it and found a soldier heaping on brush. In answer to my inquiries he said he was getting General Birney's supper. He was General Birney's cook. He said I had better stay where I was, as the brigade would all be there in a short time. I did not have to wait long, and glad enough I was to be with my regiment again.

We camped where we were over night. Our supper and breakfast consisted of salt beef, hard tack and coffee as usual. I think we did not do any fighting during the next forenoon. We had driven the enemy from our front the day before, and had had some hard fighting to do it. If the rest of the army had done as well, the Second Bull Run would have been a victory instead of a defeat. Or if McClellan had been in command of the army, it would have been a victory, as he never knew what defeat was.

In the afternoon of the second day our brigade was stationed in an open field, surrounded by woods. I saw Generals Heintzelman, Kearney and McDowell ride back and forth a number of times in our front. What they were after I could not say. Late in the afternoon we heard heavy firing on our left. Later we were ordered to retreat. As soon as we emerged from the woods, we could see that the left wing of the army had been driven back. Our brigade started to run. I threw away everything I had except my musket and equipments, as it was hard for me to keep up. We had gone but a short distance when General Kearney saw the brigade running. He said: "What! my men running?" General, speaking to General Birney, "bring your men down to quick time." They stopped running before Kearney had finished speaking. We marched a short distance, when we halted near a battery. While we were there one of the battery fired a shot into a company that was coming towards us about a quarter of a mile distant, thinking they were rebels. The company halted and told the battery to stop firing; they were our men. I did not hear of any one in the company being killed. They then came towards us.

While we were halting near the battery, a large body of men filed down near us in our front. General Kearney, thinking they were our men, rode towards them. They were rebels. The first thing he knew, he was between the rebel pickets and line of battle. But he found it out before the rebels found out who he was, and turned to come back. In coming back he came near a rebel picket, who told him to halt. He said, "Can you tell me where the —th regiment is?" naming a southern regiment he knew to be in that locality. The picket, supposing him to be a rebel officer, let him pass. So he escaped. Another of Kearney's hair breadth escapes!

While we were retreating across Bull Run, the artillery and cavalry went over the bridge, while the infantry waded through the river. The water was up to my hips. I had to hold up my cartridge box to prevent its getting wet. We marched to Centreville that night. Lieutenant Gould found a blanket in the road the next morning, and told me to get it, seeing that I had none. We stopped at Centreville two days. We could see the wounded going to the rear continually from the Bull Run battle ground; some in ambulances, some on foot, with their arms and heads tied up. I borrowed some paper and envelopes, and wrote home to my friends to let them know I was safe, as I always did after a battle. I sent the letters by a citizen, who said he would post them at Washington. I saw quite a number of citizens, who were there to see the fight. They had better have been somewhere else. One of them told us we looked as if we could fight. We made no reply to such a remark as that.

On the afternoon of the second day after we had returned to Centreville, we saw the wagons and ambulances coming back from Washington. The rebels were between us and Washington. We were ordered into line. Everyone was given the usual rounds, and the cap box filled. We expected some sort of a "brush" with the enemy, but did not expect much of a fight. One of the sergeants stepped out of the ranks, and said he thought there wouldn't be much of a fight; if he thought otherwise he would be with us. He had a lame foot. As we passed along the road we could see nice carriages broken in pieces by the rebels; they belonged to people in Washington, who had come to see the fight, and were returning.

After marching a number of miles, we filed to the left, through the woods. We could hear the racket in front, and knew we were near the battle ground. The men seemed to dread going forward more than usual. The whole company seemed to hang back. Lieutenant Gould seeing what was up, pulled out his sword and said to the sergeants, "Don't you let a man leave the ranks." He looked as though he would bite the men's heads off if they did not keep in their places. I never saw the men backward about going into a fight before. The officers talked to them, and called them cowards. One of the men stepped up to me and said, "Do you call me a coward?" "Very well, said I; then go along with your company." I told another man who held back: "You fought well at Bull Run, you can fight now." He said he was not going in there. I told him he must go with his company or there would be trouble.

The men did better after the officers had given them a good talking to. I do not think a man left the ranks. We did not have to use any force. Before we came out of the woods, it rained very hard; it was a regular thunder storm. I managed to keep the lock of my rifle dry, by putting it under my arm. Soon after we came out of the woods, we came to a house and shed. As we passed down to the left of the house to a cornfield, I heard General Kearney say, "The 38th and 40th will be in reserve." But we were not; we were in the thickest of the fight. After we reached the cornfield we commenced firing. I was well to the front; there were only a few ahead of me. I was kneeling down on my right leg, making a rest for my rifle with my left hand, my left elbow on my left knee. I had cautioned the men back of me not to hit our men in front. The men looked anxious, and had their eyes wide open. I was putting a cap on my rifle, to fire for the third time, when a ball struck my knee that was on the ground on the inside. It entered the crack of the joint diagonally, striking the knee pan, which turned it, so that it made a half circle, cracking the bone nearly to the hip, and stopping just outside of the bone. I jumped for the rear, as soon as I was hit. The wound was very painful. It seemed to shake me all over. I didn't think the men near me knew I was wounded. I said nothing to them about it. With the aid of my rifle, I managed to hop to the rear, a distance of about ten rods. I then felt tired and faint. I saw some men behind the shed, — the same house and shed we saw as we went into the fight. One of them was a sergeant of our regiment; but not of our company. I called to them to come and help me. Two of them came. I passed an arm around each of their necks, and they put their arms around my waist. We had gone but fifteen or twenty rods when we came to some men who had a stretcher. I asked them to carry me, as I was unable to go any further. At first they refused, on the ground that I did not belong to their regiment. I told them I was a wounded man, and could go no further without being carried. They finally consented to have me get on the stretcher, and carried me away. They belonged to the ambulance corps, and were just the men I wanted to see.

They cut my trousers open, and tied a bandage tightly above the wounded knee. This lessened the pain. I saw a great many of our wounded going to the rear. Some had help; others hobbled along as best they could. Our orderly sergeant, Durgin, was wounded in the hip. Seeing me, he said, "Fletcher, I would help you if I could; but I can hardly go myself."

I saw a brigadier-general with two men helping him to the rear. It was General Stevens, I suppose, who afterwards died, for he was the only brigadier general wounded in this battle..

I was carried to some buildings consisting of a house, barn and an old mule house made of logs. The mule house was full of wounded men. Our orderly sergeant was outside when I came up, and said to those inside, "Lie along. Sergeant Fletcher wants to get in there." Then I got under cover. Soon after I was put in the mule house, Lieutenant Gould was brought in, wounded in the knee. He was in great pain. He was soon after removed by some of our men. When he left, I told him to send some one for me.

He said he would, if he could. It was the rule to take care of the commissioned officers first.

After dark some surgeons came with lanterns, and took the ball from my leg. They asked me if I wanted it, and I told them I did. I carried it home with me, and lost it when I was at the G. A. R. convention at Portland, Me., in 1885.

Some time in the night, some of our officers came and said that everyone who could possibly get away, must leave. We knew then that we were to be left to the tender mercies of the rebels. I tried to crawl away into the brush, but was unable to do so. Late in the night I heard Corporal Flynn of our company talking to some one outside: I called to him, and begged of him to take care of us. At first he refused, saying he would be taken prisoner in the morning, and sent to Richmond. I told him I did not believe there would be any danger, if he tied a piece of white cloth round his arm and told the rebels that he belonged to the ambulance corps. Finally he consented to stay with us. Flynn told me that if I had read my Bible, as he had read his, before going into fight, I would not have been wounded. I wish I knew where he is now. I would give more to see him than any other man I ever knew.

We were a sober set of men that night, for we knew we should be prisoners in the morning. I myself was wet, for there had been a heavy shower before the fight. There was a fire outside the cabin, but I did not feel able to drag myself to it. A pretty fix for a man to be in; dangerously wounded, soaking wet, a prisoner in the enemy's hands, and almost out of food.

The next morning about nine o'clock, we saw a rebel cavalryman come to a knoll, a few rods from us. Soon he was joined by five or six more. Then one of them came down where we were, and looked all about the buildings, finding nothing but wounded men. Soon afterwards he was joined by the men he left on the knoll and also by some infantry that had come up in the meantime. Having placed a guard around the buildings, they proceeded to the battlefield, where they took everything they could find,—even stripping the dead.

All the rebel soldiers I saw looked well and were well armed. The cavalry rode good horses, and were armed with sabres, five-shooting carbines, and large Colts' revolvers, the same as our cavalry. A rebel colonel came into the building where we were and took all our names, to be exchanged. He said he could do nothing for us, the commissary stores not having arrived. One fellow thrust his head into the door and told us we had no business down there, anyway. We made no reply. The rebels did not take anything from us, as far as I know. We felt safe as long as the guard was there, but when this was removed, we could not help feeling uneasy. Still we were not molested,—and we stayed there a week.

After the guard left, I asked Flynn if he knew whether any of our company had been killed or wounded. He told me he saw a man by the name of Wiley coming to the rear with his hand on his breast, and that afterwards he had found his dead body; that all the commissioned officers and sergeants had been killed or disabled, and that a corporal had commanded the company. Besides, many of the privates were killed. Chantilly was a Gettysburg for our company, and in fact was a most severe fight for all engaged. The 21st Mass. lost more men in this battle than in any other during the whole war.

When we had been prisoners a few days, our rations gave out. Flynn dug the garden over two or three times, and cooked for us all the potatoes, beets, turnips or other eatables he could find. I was always served first. Two surgeons were left to take charge of us, but we did not have our wounds dressed till the fourth day after the fight. The surgeons told us they had been busy day and night since the battle. There were about one hundred and fifty wounded men in the buildings where we were; five or six died of their wounds every twenty-four hours. Flynn and the other well men buried them. None died in the cabin where I was; the worst cases were in the house.

Flynn stayed with us till we went away. I have not seen or heard from him since. I have sometimes thought he might have been taken prisoner after we left, and carried to Richmond.

The next morning after we had been taken prisoners, the rebels told us that they had killed "that one-armed devil, General Kearney." We told them we did not believe it. One poor fellow, who lay next to me, had a very painful wound in his instep. He and I agreed to go away together, if we could. After the first twelve hours, my wound did not pain me. I washed it from time to time, and tried to keep it as cool as possible. The first man to dress the wound was a volunteer surgeon. He put round it some nice, clean cloth, which made it feel much more comfortable. He said he was going away a short distance to where the rebel wounded were to get a canteen to carry home as a relic. He said he would see me again when we reached Washington, and he kept his promise.

The last few days we had very little to eat except coffee. The agents of the Sanitary Commission were the first to find us; and then we had bread in abundance. I ate so much bread and coffee that I made myself sick. The agent was very kind to us; he said he would have come to us before, if he had known where we were. One day, late in the afternoon, after we had been prisoners about a week, we saw an ambulance standing in front of the door of our pen. We thought we were going away, sure; but I was mistaken. I made up my mind, if another ambulance cart came, to get into it, if possible, for I had been there long enough.

## CHAPTER XIII.

#### HOSPITAL LIFE.

The next morning an ambulance came and stood before the door again. I crawled to the door, and with the assistance of a man who was standing near, managed to get into the ambulance. There were some thirty ambulances in the train, each drawn by two horses. There were two wounded men in each, lying on beds. The ambulances extended out over the wheels, so that we had plenty of room.

The agent of the Sanitary Commission accompanied us to Washington, and very kindly furnished us with wine and brandy and water. We started from the prison pen about four o'clock in the afternoon, and arrived in Washington about dawn the next day. I did not sleep much, I was placed in the Cliffborn Hospital. Clean clothes were given us, and we were washed for the first time for a week.

The ward surgeon looked at my wound the first thing in the morning, and told me the leg would have to come off. I did not like that very well. The head surgeon examined the wound and wanted to know if I felt well. I told him "first rate, all but the wound." He said he would try to save the limb, and had it bathed night and day in ice water. Cliffborn Hospital was situated about three miles east or north east of the city.

Immediately upon my arrival in Washington, I wrote to several of my friends at home to let them know what had happened to me. I asked my brother, Theodore, to come to me as soon as he should receive my letter, for I wanted to see some one I knew. The letter was delayed somewhere. He did not arrive in Washington till a week after my limb had been amputated, about the 25th of September. He received the letter one morning and started for Washington in the afternoon. My wound did not pain me from the time of my arrival at the hospital till the amputation. On the 18th of September I was not feeling as well as usual. Later in the afternoon a surgeon came to me and said they were going to examine my limb, and if necessary amputate it. I told them to go ahead. A sponge saturated with ether was put to my nostrils, and soon I was unconscious. When I came to, it was candle light; two nurses were standing by me, one on each side of the bed. The first thing I heard was, "Why don't you wake up, Fletcher?" They were pinching my nose and ears. I told them to let me alone. I had no feeling in my hands or feet; could talk, but could not stir. I felt no pain. But very soon I did feel a terrible pain at the end of the stump, and told the nurses they must do something to relieve it. They said they would in a short time; they wanted to wait till the ether had left me. In due time I was given something which relieved the pain, but I did not sleep much that first night, and when I did sleep I was dreaming all the time.

The surgeon did not remove the bandage from the stump for two days after the amputation, and he found it badly dried on to the flesh, so that it took him a long time to take it off. When a leg is amputated, about a dozen little arteries have to be tied up with little strings and left two or three inches long. Some twelve or thirteen days after a limb is amputated these strings drop off of their own accord. Fifteen days after my leg was taken off the surgeon found one of the strings still on the wound, and was somewhat alarmed. He pulled it off, however, without disturbing the artery. I suffered considerable pain, and was obliged to take morphine every night to make me sleep. I usually felt pretty comfortable in the morning, however. I had to lie on my back all the time. The wound was very slow in healing, and my appetite was poor. I lived on milk punch and two bottles of London porter a day. For two or three weeks my brother, Theodore, came to see me every day for a little while, and most of the time on Sundays. He then was obliged to go home to make arrangements for his fall work, but soon came back again.

For a week or more the surgeon dressed the wound, and then the ward master. None of the nurses could dress it without giving me great pain. The stump was not doing well; it would not heal; great ulcers formed which the surgeon lanced, giving me much pain. I dreaded to see him every morning, and was glad when he left me. He said he wanted I should eat something, and told me I could have anything I wanted. When Theodore came back, he brought me some splended peaches, which I was very glad to eat. A few days later a wounded man in the hospital ate some fruit which turned his stomach. The exertion of vomiting caused him to burst an artery, so that he bled to death. The head surgeon after that gave orders that no more fruit should be brought into the hospital. I had quite a number of peaches left, but did not eat any more.

One day the ward master told me that there was another man in the hospital whose thigh had been amputated in about the same place as mine, and that he was in about the same condition that I was. "Now, let me see," he said, "who is the best fellow." Every morning they told me his condition. After a number of days I was told he was not doing well; he would not lie still, and this made bad work with his stump. He was finally tied to the bed post, but even then he could not be kept quiet. One morning the surgeon told me the poor fellow had died during the night. Out of seven or eight in my ward whose thighs had been amputated I was the only one left alive. Every morning the surgeon told me to keep still. I obeyed him as well I could, but it was terribly hard.

The Cliffborn Hospital was made up of twelve wards, each containing eighty patients. The bed clothing consisted of a mattress, pillow, white sheets and woolen blankets. The patients lay on single beds, with their heads towards the wall on both sides of the building. A passage way at their feet ran the whole length of the room. There was plenty of space between the beds for the nurses to pass around among the patients. There was a surgeon over the whole hospital, and, besides, there was a surgeon for each ward. One evening about nine o'clock, after I had been in the hospital about a month, the ward master sent two nurses to rub my back. After they had left me my wound pained me more than usual, and I made so much noise on account of the pain that the ward master heard me. On being told what the trouble was he said: "I knew those fellows would not leave your stump right." He then took hold of it with both hands and placed it in a different position, and I was instantly relieved.

There was a man lying near me whose leg had been amputated about like mine. It was said he had five wounds in his body and limbs. The surgeon was trying to get up his strength so that his arm could be amputated. He had been on the bed four weeks. I then thought that I could not lie on my back four weeks, but I did lie three months. The ward master took great pains with this patient, calling him a plucky fellow. One afternoon he asked for a cigar. It was given him, and he seemed to enjoy it very much. The same evening I heard him say: "I can't stand it." He died during the night. The man lying on my left who had had his arm amputated, also died. The surgeon said there was nothing the matter with him. He simply worried himself to death. He had a wife and several children at home.

The Sanitary Commission Agents of the different states came to the hospital to look after the patients coming from their respective states. The agent from New York kindly offered to assist me, though I came from Massachusetts, and though the Massachusetts agent had previously made arrangements to get certain things for me. These agents furnished us with bandages, lint, writing material, postage stamps, or anything else we needed. The Massachusetts agent gave me his address and told me to send for him if I wanted anything. One morning, when my wound was being dressed, it was found that there was no lint or bandages in the hospital. I sent word to the agent, and in the afternoon received from him a large box full of lint. At the request of the ward master I furnished lint for some of the worst cases. They had to tear up good sheets for bandages. It took four or five men to take me off the bed when the bed clothes were changed. They had me sit by the stove, wrapped up in blankets. They did this a number of times, but finally had to give it up, for the exertion was too much for me. I was not allowed to read and had to keep perfectly quiet, a very difficult thing to do. One evening one of the convalescent patients had a box from home full of good things. Several ate these good things at the foot of my bed—to tempt me to eat something I suppose. Among other things they had baked potatoes and boiled onions. The next morning I asked for baked potatoes and boiled onions, which were sent to me, together with a juicy steak. That was the first time I had eaten anything that I relished for about three weeks. After that I ate more and drank less London porter and milk punch. The porter, by the way, was taken from me all at once,—a thing which I did not like very well, for I had been having it every day for several weeks. So I had my brother bring me a bottle when he came from Washington. I put it in the bed so that the nurse could not see it. I soon stopped drinking it, however.

The Sisters of Charity had charge of the worst cases in the hospital. When a soldier died the face of some sister was the last thing he saw in this world. The one who attended to me used to come the first thing in the morning and bathe my face with bay rum. She then would comb my hair and give me milk punch or anything else that I wanted to eat. She called to see me a number of times in the course of the day. One afternoon when I was very low I told the sister that I was going to get some crutches and come down to meet her in the morning. I wanted to take my mind from the terrible condition I was in, if possible. That night I was told to say my prayers. When the attendants came in the morning they stood at the bed a few moments to see if I was alive. The sister came quickly to the head of the bed and said: "Mr. Fletcher, I thought you were coming to meet me this morning on crutches." She said it in such a pleasant way that I almost forgot that I was sick. I told her that I had put it off till some future day.

One day the sister asked me if I had been christened. I told her I had. Every morning and night I sent up an earnest petition to the Almighty to help our cause, to enable us to put down the rebellion and to permit me to live to see the end of the war. I felt stronger after offering my prayers. Perhaps they saved my life. I fear I did not pray very much when I had a sound body and good rifle, and plenty of powder and balls. At all events, I called on my Maker to help me and our cause, when I could do nothing to help the cause of the Union myself. All my wishes were gratified, and I fully believe that the Almighty was on our side. At times I had spells of crying like a child. I was in great distress, and there was not much prospect of being any better. At such times I would cover up my face with the sheet so that no one could see me.

At one time one of the men who was able to be about accused the sister of stealing his pipe, and used abusive language to her. He was tried by court martial and sentenced to have a shower bath, which was considered a severe punishment. The sister interfered in his behalf and had him released.

All the nurses in the hospital, except the Sisters of Charity, were United States soldiers. The surgeons, also, belonged to the army. Finally the ward master got out of patience with me. I had been confined to my bed for two months or more and did not seem to get any better or worse. One morning he had hold of my stump with both hands, when he raised it about two inches and let it drop suddenly and said: "Fletcher you will neither live nor die." My leg pained me terribly, and if I had been able to get up, I should have been tempted to knock him down. At another time a consultation on my case was held by three surgeons, the ward surgeon, the surgeon of the hospital and another surgeon still higher in authority, I thought, though I did not know who he was. They stood at the foot of my bed talking and looking at me. I was very low at the time and my eyes were closed. The surgeon of the hospital said: "Fletcher, look up at me. Your eyes look bright. I'll venture they can't kill you with a sledge hammer." As they stood there talking, a man they called "Stumpy," came along and asked the head surgeon if he could not go home. "Go home!" said the surgeon, "What do you want to go home for? to go on a drunk? No! Stay where you are." Poor "Stumpy" didn't say any more.

"Stumpy" was a soldier who had had his arm amputated above the elbow. The stump did not pain him, but the part that was gone did, and there was no way to relieve him. His stump healed very well. I do not know what became of him, for I was so low and week at the time that I did not inquire. The nurses and others in the hospital laughed at him a good deal, because he said that the part of the arm that was gone pained him.

One day a large, heavy soldier whose thigh had been amputated much as mine had been, came to see me. He was on crutches and said he had been confined to his bed but four weeks. The wound had not completely healed but was very comfortable, and the man looked well. One day the ward master was taken sick. We all felt his absence very much, especially myself, for none of the nurses could do as well as he. At one time no one but he could dress my wound without giving me great pain.

The last of December, 1862, my brother, Theodore, said he would have to go home. I was much better but still confined to my bed. I said I was going with him. The nurses in the ward said I would never live to get there.

I asked Theodore to consult the head surgeon about the matter. He said it would not hurt me at all, but would do me good. I tried to get a furlough. The authorities were ready to give me my discharge, but not a furlough. A week before I started for home I was moved to another hospital, called Lincoln Hospital. One morning while I was there, a man was brought in who had lost his foot by amputation. He heard me speak and then called me by name. I did not recognize him at first. It was Booth of our company. He wanted to know how I was getting along. I told him "First rate," but had had a distressing time of it to pull through. He was getting better. His mother came out to see him after he arrived at the hospital. It was he that I spoke of as being wounded at Bull Run, at the time when the lieutenant would not let me go back and help him to the rear. He recovered and afterwards lived at Philadelphia. When I left for home the surgeons asked me to write and let them know how I stood the journey.

I had to lie on a bed all the way. We went in the cars to New York, and then took the boat to Fall River, and then the cars again to Boston. Theodore managed to get my discharge papers after trying for about a week. He had to get papers from my company, and then go to half a dozen different places in Washington before everything was arranged. I obtained an equivalent for those things that I was entitled to and had not received.

On our way home we had to cross the Susquehannah at Havre de Grace on a ferry boat. I was placed near a stove, where it was warm. There was quite a number of ladies on board the boat. Before we had crossed the river some called out, "There lies a Union soldier who has lost his leg in the war." Some of the ladies held their handkerchiefs to their faces, and I could see tears in their eyes as they looked at me.

At Philadelphia I bought an air bed of a man who had lost both feet. His home was in this city; so he had no further use for it. I found this bed much more comfortable than the one I had. On the boat from New York I was placed near the stove, so as to keep warm. Theodore secured a mattress and lay down near me. He gave me some morphine, which had been furnished by the hospital, and I slept fairly well. Still I awoke several times, and I always found Theodore sitting up on his mattress, looking at me. He wanted to see how I was getting along, he said. I told him I was all right, and advised him to go to sleep.

At Fall River we missed a train. There was another wounded man traveling on a bed, and he was put on the train first. I had just been brought into the station, when the train started out. Missing the train made it necessary for us to stay in Boston over night, so that we did not reach home until January 2. We arrived in Boston soon after dark, New Year's Day, 1863. We passed the night very comfortably at a hotel; after supper we had a long talk about the war and country, and various other things.

In order to have plenty of time we did not start from Boston till the second train. The Fitchburg Railroad, for our special benefit, attached to the train a freight car with a stove in it. They did not make any extra charge. Arriving at the railroad station in Boston, the first man I saw from Littleton was Deacon Hall. I took my hand from under the bed clothes to shake hands with him. "Don't take your hand out. You will take cold," he said. I told him I was going to shake hands with him anyway.

I made the journey to West Acton very comfortably, and was carried from the station there to my brother's in an express wagon. I had been in the United States' Army for the suppression of the Rebellion one year and six months, lacking one day. I was in the following battles: The siege of Yorkstown, Williamsburg, Fair Oak, Peach Orchard, Savage Station, White Oak Swamp, Glendale, Malvern Hill, first and second Bull Run, and Chantilly.

# CONCLUSION.

## MY ESTIMATE OF GENERAL MCCLELLAN.

In my opinion General George B. McClellan was the best general this country has produced, with the exception of Washington. Not only was he a great general, but he was a true patriot as well.

When the war broke out, he was president of the Baltimore & Mississippi Railroad, with a salary of $10,000 a year. He had recently married, and had a very pleasant home. He left all, however, to fight for his country.

After his brilliant campaign in West Virginia, he was appointed to command all the armies of the United States. His services to his country in organizing the Army of the Potomac cannot be overestimated, and for this alone he would be entitled to the gratitude of future ages.

In the spring of 1855 the general government sent three officers, of whom McClellan was one, to Europe, to study the changes made in military science, and to report on those changes. They were instructed to pay attention to every detail of the whole art of war.

The British Government extended to them every courtesy. From the French and Russians, however, they could obtain no facilities. They were received in the Crimea with soldierly kindness by General Simpson, the

British commander. Here they had ample opportunity for the study of military operations on a grand scale.

Leaving the Crimea in November these American officers visited the various European states, examining very many military posts and fortifications noted in history. McClellan's report, in the words of a distinguished soldier, was "a model of conciseness and accurate information," and added to his already brilliant reputation.

Of McClellan's campaign in West Virginia, his organization of the Army of the Potomac, and his appointment as general-in-chief, we have already spoken. Under his leadership we have the victories of New Orleans, Fort Pulaska, victories in North Carolina under Burnside, capture of Forts Henry and Donaldson by Grant, the taking of Nashville and the Battle of Shiloh, the Peninsular Campaign and the Battle of Antietam. He had to fight the rebel army when it was in its prime, and always defeated it.

After the battle of Second Bull Run, when the President thought of putting Burnside in command of the Army of the Potomac, Burnside remarked that he could not handle so large an army, and that no one could so well as McClellan.

General O. O. Howard, upon hearing of the removal of McClellan, expressed his surprise and extreme regret. Howard was in the Peninsular Campaign, and lost an arm at Fair Oaks.

General A. P. Martin said McClellan would have ended the war in 1862, if he had not been removed from the command of the army.

General McClellan was very popular with both officers and men, and he had the rare quality of discovering the abilities of his officers. In fact, Colonel Clark, Commissary of the Army of the Potomac, General Hunt, Chief of Artillery, and Colonel Ingalls, Chief of Quartermaster, all of whom were appointed by McClellan, served in their respective positions till the close of the war.

One day McClellan saw Lieutenant G. A. Custer, of the 5th U. S. Cavalry, manœuvre on the field of battle, and was so much pleased with his operations that he put him on his staff.

General Meade was promoted after Antietam at the suggestion of McClellan.

McClellan always looked out for the privates, and did not have them make forced marches, or do anything else that was disagreeable, until the President interferred.

McClellan was careful to look out for everything himself. During the Seven Days' Fight he was in the saddle most of the time, day and night. In a private letter to his wife, at this time, he writes: "I am all but tired out. No sleep for two nights and none to-night."

McClellan's plan in 1862 was to go to Richmond by way of the Peninsular with an army of 150,000 men and 600 cannon, draw there most of the rebel forces, fight one big battle and end the war at once. In the opinion of the best military critics he would have succeeded, had he not been interfered with by the authorities at Washington. In fact, John T. Morse, Jr., in his "Life of Lincoln," admits that if McDowell had reinforced McClellan instead of going on a wild goose chase after Stonewall Jackson in the Shenandoah Valley, McClellan would probably have succeeded.

Gen. Sherman was a warm admirer of McClellan. In a letter to his brother, Senator Sherman, dated Feb. 23, 1862, he says: "Don't make war on McClellan. You mistake him if you underrate him." In January, 1863, Gen. Sherman again writes: "You have driven off McClellan. Is Burnside any better?" Again in February, 1863, he writes: "The press have now killed McClellan, Buell, Fitz-John Porter, Sumner, Franklin, and Burnside. Add my name and I am not ashamed of the association."

McClellan made everybody work, and he worked himself. When we were not on the march we had to drill. After a long march we usually rested a day, consequently the troops were always in good condition for a fight.

Many thought McClellan was slow in moving his army, but no one has any idea of the amount of work there was to drill, arm and equip the Army of the Potomac. McClellan started on the Peninsular Campaign about two months sooner than Grant did his campaign in 1864. No general could accomplish much in winter in Virginia on account of rain and mud.

No general did more for the Union cause than "Little Mac," and he should stand first among our generals in the heart of every true American.

www.ingramcontent.com/pod-product-compliance
Lightning Source LLC
Chambersburg PA
CBHW020840160426
43192CB00007B/724